Larry

Best of luck with
the medin Sector

30/Sept 09

Enterprise*

*The leadership role

Roger Parry

*Enterprise**

*The leadership role

P

PROFILE BOOKS

First published in Great Britain in 2003 by
Profile Books Ltd
58A Hatton Garden
London EC1N 8LX
www.profilebooks.co.uk

Typeset in Lapidary 333 by MacGuru
info@macguru.org.uk

Printed and bound in Great Britain by
Clays, Bungay, Suffolk

A CIP catalogue record for this book is available from the British Library.

ISBN 1 86197 634 8

To Benjamin

ENTERPRISE: bold adventure
initiative
daring spirit
a venture
a joint stock undertaking
a business concern

The Oxford English Dictionary
The New Webster's Dictionary

Contents

Figures and tables

Figures

Tables

Acknowledgements

In writing this book I owe a great debt to work colleagues past and present. The BBC taught me the value of making the complex simple to understand. McKinsey & Co. did for me what it does for many – providing analytical rigour to base decisions on facts, not emotion. Many years spent working in advertising and media companies have shown me that clear communication – external and internal – is crucial in a society overloaded with information. I have found I have learned from most people and, probably, been very ungracious in not recognising that. Please accept my amends now.

I am currently in the very fortunate position of overseeing businesses in more than fifty countries and thus am able to work with a large number of talented and very different managers. I have learned far more from them than from any book or lecture. I have to thank my colleagues at Clear Channel for putting up with my distractions during the research and writing, and for responding to my many questions about their take on various management ideas.

My colleagues who are or were CEOs of companies where I am or have been a director may well recognise some of their ideas in this book. In particular many thanks to Charles, Colin, Coline, Crispin, Greg, Jacques, Lowry, Mark, Peter, Tim and Wayne.

I must thank Charles Peattie and Russell Taylor who caused *Alex* to make a special guest cartoon appearance in this book and also to Knight Features for the cartoon on page xi. Thanks also to Jerry Useem of *Fortune* magazine who shared his thoughts with me on the development of CEO styles, and to Jim Collins for allowing me to quote from his work on vision and corporate success. The editors of the *Harvard Business Review* have been particularly generous in allowing me to use extracts from their archive.

Martin Liu at Profile Books was brave enough to commission this book and has restructured it to make it a far better read. His colleagues Penny Daniel and Trevor Horwood turned my poor grammar into English, but any mistakes that remain are mine.

My apologies also to my wife and son for my vanishing for many hours at weekends, closeted with my PC. My son is now so far ahead of me on most games on X Box and PlayStation that I have no chance of catching up. I am grateful to Michael Earl, the Dean of Templeton College Oxford, and to his staff for the use of their library. I must thank British Airways and Eurostar, in whose lounges and seats much of this book was written.

My special thanks to my assistant and friend Zarina, who has kept up my morale and sorted out the endless and ongoing mess I created in writing this book. Also for designing the diagrams and chasing up all the copyright permissions. Without her help the book would never have been published.

Introduction

Businesses exist to create wealth for their owners – their shareholders. But they do this through creating value for their customers, generating cash and keeping many other responsibilities in balance.

It was a relentless and over-enthusiastic pursuit of the cult of *shareholder value* alone that led to many of the recent corporate disasters. Chief executives – CEOs – are now expected to display a wider range of skills and styles. They have to be more flexible in their thinking and more rounded in their approach. More *Renaissance Man* than *Attila the Hun*, more tightrope walker than master magician.

An *organisation* is a way of grouping people together to achieve common objectives. An *enterprise* is an organisation which moves forwards, takes risks, creates value and rewards the capital invested in it. Successful CEOs do more than just achieve a temporary increase in the share price. They make their businesses true enterprises, not just organisations, by providing both leadership and management.

The raging bull stock markets of the 1990s created the myth of CEO as superstar. Accounting scandals, remuneration controversies and business collapses have led to a fundamental reappraisal. Trying to understand this new role of the CEO and how it relates to corporate success or failure is why this book has been written.

Some businesses thrive in what are generally thought to be poor industries. Others crash into losses or bankruptcy when their industry itself is prospering. Many companies – particularly in technology and telecoms – have gone 'up like a rocket' and down like the proverbial 'stick' whilst others turn out consistent growth year after year. What differentiates the winners from the losers?

Corporate success in this book is defined as achieving a better long-term return on capital than an average investment. But there is no one single management button to push or commercial lever to pull to achieve this.

Businesses with the most brilliant strategy will fail without good implementation. And CEOs who are long on theory and short on delivery will, nowadays, end up out of a job. However, no amount of energy and effort can overcome a doomed business model. Even the most talented, hands-on people can put in long hours but see their companies fail if the basic economics are wrong. Some very good managers went down with the dot.com ships.

Business success is based on doing a number of things well, consistently, over a long period of time. It is about understanding what is really going on in a company and setting the right priorities. This means it is disproportionately about the performance of the individual who has to set the tasks, find the people to do them and keep the pressure up for performance every day – the CEO.

This is not to suggest that CEOs are some sort of superheroes who leap corporate hurdles at a single bound, nor that they are the sole reason that businesses succeed or fail. It is simply that they must do a good job of being the leader and that their role is different from other managers in a company.

This book is not about 'what it takes to be a CEO' but about how successful CEOs behave. It is not a 'how to' manual, nor does it offer an off-the-shelf 'management concept' or revolutionary new formula. *Enterprise* poses questions about what businesses really are and how they work. It then describes ten actions which, when performed well by the CEO, drive business success.

The ideas in *Enterprise* come from working with, and learning from, outstanding business leaders, from management colleagues, academics, investment analysts and business journalists, and from personal experience. I do not pretend that all the ideas in this book are original, or that they are the only approach. But these principles of how to think about business success have worked for me and seem to work for others.

If there is a simple way of describing the new style of CEO for the twenty-first century it is about bringing out the best in others. The days of the dominating, charismatic, over-the-top leader are gone but the role of good management and inspiring leadership is as important as ever in turning businesses into thriving enterprises

Part I of *Enterprise* describes the evolution of the CEO role in the context of the development of companies over the past few hundred years. As the needs of shareholders have changed so the role and style of management have also altered. The excesses of the 1990s boom developed out of the ideas of momentum investing, financial engineering and an extreme interpretation of shareholder value creation. We are all living with the consequences. Dramatic corporate failures have led to demands for the development of a new style of top management.

Part II outlines the role of the CEO in achieving the transformation from organisation to enterprise. Drawing on the classic theories of management, accepted current best practice and using real-life examples, it describes the ten actions which need to be performed well if the business is to thrive:

- Defining the business – vision
- Setting clear goals – strategy
- Ensuring accountability – structure
- Finding talent – people
- Delegating authority – tactics
- Operating effectively – generating cash
- Moving forward – managing change
- Picking winners – finding high-return investments
- Managing transactions – making deals work
- Telling the story well – internal and external communications.

I did not write this book thinking that I know all the solutions to the challenges that face CEOs. Indeed from my own experience it is clear there are no easy answers. This book is about how to ask the right questions more than prescribing the perfect actions.

Readers looking for insights from proven leaders will enjoy biographies such as those of Lou Gerstner and Jack Welch. Those looking for groundbreaking new management concepts will find them in the work of writers like Jim Collins and Michael Porter. *Enterprise* has the modest aim of drawing from sources like these, both practical and theoretical, to provide insights and provoke discussion.

I have learned a lot about the role of the CEO from being employed as one and from being a non-executive chairman watching others do the hard work. I have also talked to management experts and read their views. Of course, it is all very well to sit back making observations and suggesting theories, but getting it right in practice is another matter altogether.

What is clear is that there are widespread demands for a new approach to the top job. Investors, legislators, employees and customers want to see corporate leadership that is more practical and pragmatic and that creates real value in a business over the long term. *Enterprise* is a contribution to the development of a new set of management principles designed to achieve a more balanced approach to running a company aimed at creating lasting value.

Part I

EVOLUTION OF THE CEO

CEOs are supposed to build and lead companies, create value, generate employment and make shareholders rich. So what went so horribly wrong in the past few years? Take this list:

WorldCom: $107 billion
Enron: $63 billion
Vivendi: $14 billion
Tyco: $90 billion.[1]

These are big numbers. The figures against the first two are the damage suffered when they filed for bankruptcy protection – the largest corporate failures in history. Vivendi's is the largest annual loss in French records, reported after writing down investments. Tyco's is the sudden slump in that company's market value after investors realised that 'the Emperor had no clothes'.

All these businesses thrived – or appeared to – during the 1990s boom. All collapsed as a result of deeply flawed leadership, over-aggressive expansion and hopeless corporate governance. These were huge destructions of investor wealth – exactly the opposite of the philosophy, almost the cult, of shareholder value that led to companies like these being built up in the first place. The boom also led to the huge remuneration and near deification of some CEOs. What happened to make the reality so different from the dream?

WorldCom made hundreds of acquisitions, which hid its true operating results. When regulations forced the acquisition process to stop, the house of cards collapsed. But by then its board had agreed to lend its own CEO Bernie Ebbers more than $400 million, which in part helped him to buy a ranch in Canada and some 500,000 acres of forest.[2]

Enron operated a range of off-balance-sheet vehicles (i.e. their debts were concealed), which gave the impression of earnings whilst hiding liabilities. Its accounts, which were audited by the then industry-leading Arthur Andersen and approved by its impressive board of directors, showed profits much higher than they really were. This helped the CEO and other senior executives sell hundreds of millions of dollars' worth of personally owned shares at high prices before the crash.

Vivendi paid breathtaking amounts to acquire entertainment assets and then failed to make them work coherently together. Its CEO, the Napoleonic Jean-Marie Messier, who had used debt to turn a French water and sewage business into a global entertainment empire, persuaded the company to buy him a $17-million New York apartment to go with his new-found status of world media mogul.[3]

Tyco made many good deals but its leaders began to get ludicrously greedy. In prosecuting Dennis Kozlowski, the fallen CEO, the Manhattan District Attorney Robert M. Morgenthau cited thirty-eight felony counts totalling more than $500 million, which included the now infamous $6,000 gold-inlay shower curtain and the $15,000 poodle-shaped umbrella stand the company bought to keep its CEO happy. The Manhattan DA observed that 'In the past crooks tended to act on their own. Now you've got a lot of people involved, and that's lawyers, accountants, executives, the board of directors. The whole system seems to have broken down.'[4]

The long stock market boom in the USA and Europe at the end of the last century created conditions in which investors started to believe in the financially impossible. The New Economy seemed to perform magic. The economic rationale looked more like something from J. K. Rowling than from J. K. Galbraith. This made capital too easily available, boards too complacent, and encouraged CEOs to became rock stars. Businesses, investors and regulators lost the plot. Senior executives became obscenely wealthy.

Commenting on the late-1990s mania, anthropologist Michael Maccoby said, 'Given the large number of narcissists at the helm of corporations today the challenge facing organisations is to ensure that such leaders do not self-destruct or lead the company to disaster.'[5]

At the end of the last millennium the Anglo-Saxon version of corporate capitalism was tried, tested and found wanting. The philosophy of shareholder value produced exactly the opposite of its objectives. Management got rich. Shareholders got screwed. This has led to fundamental questions about the role of CEOs.

The second part of this book describes the approach now required of CEOs and the ten actions they need to keep in balance to achieve success. But before that, Part I looks at the background to the new thinking by asking two questions:

- What is a business?
- What is a CEO?

1   What is a business?

*The modern corporation developed out of the joint stock
company of the sixteenth century, which was a mechanism for
shareholders to own a business whilst limiting their risks. It was
also a framework within which they could employ professional
managers. Businesses have to serve their customers and many
other stakeholders in order to increase the wealth of their
owners. The true value of a business is the sum of all the cash it
will generate in the future.*

The role of CEO results directly from the development of modern business structures. It is not possible to understand how the top job came about without explaining the context of what businesses really are, how they work and why they exist.

Most of us who work do so in a business. Companies employ us. We are part of organisations. But most of us do not ask a lot of questions about what these structures really are, where they come from and how they function. We just drift into corporate life without thinking too much about how it came to be this way. To understand why businesses succeed or fail we need to ask some basic questions about what a company really is. The co-founder of Hewlett-Packard, David Packard, said:

> A group of people get together and exist as an
> institution that we call a company so they are able to
> accomplish something collectively that they could not
> accomplish separately.[1]

A business is an organisation designed to make a profit. It creates goods or services which customers are prepared to pay for. It is an organisational device to allow investors to get a better return on their money than if they had left it in a bank. A business enterprise normally takes the legal form of a company, which is owned by shareholders, run by managers and employs people who do things to serve customers. This chapter provides context to the role of CEO through the answers to four basic questions:

1 Why do companies exist?
2 Who does a company serve?
3 What is 'success' for a company?
4 How much is a company worth?

The answers to these questions provide a common language for the later analysis of the CEO's role.

Why do companies exist?

Businesses, be they large or small, are organisations set up and operated to create wealth for their shareholders. They do this if customers are prepared to pay more for goods and services than it costs the company to supply them. Businesses also create employment and may provide other benefits to society. But the reason they exist is to make money for their owners.

The assertions in the above paragraph are open to challenge. Some might say there are different, fundamental, reasons for businesses to exist. It has been argued that the main role of a business is to provide employment; or that shareholders should only get returns after employees and government have taken their share of wealth creation; or that environmental and social responsibilities must come before profits.

Lest there be any doubt, this book is based on the premise that the main reason for a company to exist is to create shareholder wealth, which normally follows from achieving profitable growth. Governments can then decide how they will tax that shareholder wealth and how employees and the environment should be legally protected.

However, the most successful businesses also recognise their other commitments and take account of the needs of all their 'stakeholders' whilst ensuring that the legitimate needs of their owners, their shareholders, come first.

Origins of the joint stock company

The task of our ancient ancestors was either hunting or farming. It quickly became desirable for the hunters and the farmers to trade – meat for potatoes, hides for bread. And it was then only a matter of time before lawyers and investment bankers emerged from the primeval swamps to manage the transactions.

Before the invention of money, trade was simple and corporate structures unnecessary. Bargains were struck; goods changed hands at mutually agreed exchange rates. Gold and silver, as rare and precious metals, become used as a store of value and could be swapped for goods. Even after money came along, most traders were individuals or families; if they wanted something they paid in cash and kept the coins under the bed.

What really created companies, then, was not just the need for a corporate trading system. It was also the need to borrow money.

Lending money to an individual was straightforward. The borrower was responsible for the debt and had to pay it no matter what happened to their business. It was an onerous, individual obligation. Those wanting to know how Shakespeare saw the issue in 1596 should read *The Merchant of Venice* to discover what might have happened to Antonio when he got on the wrong side of Shylock after being unable to repay his personal debts.

In fact by the late sixteenth century people across Europe were regularly making use of early forms of corporate structures to keep their own skin intact. The concept of the joint stock company was a way for a group of people to come together to pay for an enterprise and share in its success. It meant simply that a business was jointly owned with each person holding some of the stock or shares. If the business went wrong, the investors lost their original money but they could not be forced to put more in. Their personal pound of flesh was not on the line.

Very typically, many of the expeditions from Europe to the New World were financed by groups of rich nobles but actually carried out by, often penniless, adventurers. The nobles had no wish to endure a long and dangerous sea voyage and they hired professionals to face the rigours of the ocean, thus introducing the concept of paid management. Also, they did not wish to be at risk for more than their initial investment if the whole thing went under – the concept of limited liability. Walter Raleigh, who popularised tobacco, and Christopher Columbus, who discovered America, were financed by early versions of joint stock companies. Without the joint stock company we would probably never have had the Marlboro Cowboy.

Shakespeare himself was very familiar with the idea of corporate ownership and his Globe Theatre was financed by selling parts of the business to 'sharers' who put up the cash to build it and would get a share of the profits – if any. But even back then the big-name entrepreneurs did not necessarily make their shareholders any money.

Alongside the concept of ownership by *shareholders* and operation by *managers* came the profession of accountancy in order to keep score. To prevent their managers cheating them, shareholders wanted to see record books and to have an accurate statement of profit and assets. The annual audit and the Report and Accounts came into use.

This corporate structure allowed people to come together to take business risks without putting their whole lives on the line, but of course meant that it was less attractive – as an individual trader – to do business with a limited company. If a company owed you money you might not get paid if the company failed. At least you could claim the home and possessions of any individual who owed you money. This led to the concept of creditworthiness and the emergence of ratings agencies to assess which corporations were acceptable customers.

As people became richer and family skills and energy were not always inherited along with money, the separation between shareholders (who owned the business) and managers (who ran it) become more distinct, but it was not really until the great industrial age of the nineteenth century that the modern idea of the third-party investor became firmly established.

John D. Rockefeller put the Standard Oil Company together through a series of acquisitions in the late nineteenth century. It made him the richest man in the world but he also become the target of many government inspired 'trust-busting' plans. In the 1890s, although not yet sixty years old, Rockefeller decided to step back from daily involvement in the company. In his analysis of Rockefeller author David Gross comments:

> In the ultimate expression of the *new* distinction
> between management and ownership that Rockefeller
> had pioneered, he and his entire generation of
> associates gradually left the business in the hands of a
> younger group of salaried executives with proven
> managerial mettle.[2]

The emphasis on the *new* is mine, as it illustrates the point that as recently as 1890 the concept of splitting ownership from day-to-day management was a relatively novel idea.

A hundred years ago a company's main full-time officer – unusually the chairman or president – was also often its largest shareholder. As businesses developed, becoming larger and more complex, more authority was shifted from shareholders to managers.

Increasingly corporate owners were investment institutions, not individuals, and the role of the CEO became even more central and powerful.

The dominating role and huge remuneration of today's chief executives is a direct result of the development of professional investment firms. This marked the ultimate separation of ownership and management. The recent surge of interest in shareholder rights and corporate governance is a realisation by professional investors that management were becoming too focused on their own enrichment and leaving their shareholders a poor second.

Who does a company serve?

A company has to take account of the views of a number of constituencies. These are people or groups of people who have some sort of 'stake' in the company and who have a legitimate interest in its progress. The stakeholders in a company include:

- shareholders (who provide capital by buying shares),
- customers (those who buy its products or services),
- employees (those who work for it and manage it),
- bankers (who provide loans of cash),
- suppliers (who provide goods and services),
- government (which regulates its operations and collects taxes).

It is from the successful interaction between itself and these groups that a company creates wealth.

A CEO must also communicate with other related groups – secondary constituencies – who represent, or act as channels to, the main stakeholders. These include:

- the board of management,
- auditors,

Figure 1.1   **The CEO manages the stakeholders**

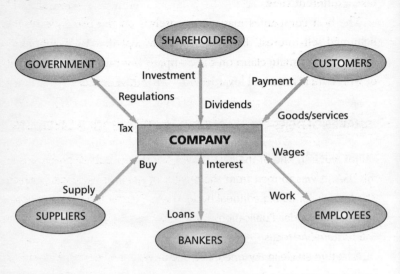

- the media,
- politicians,
- trade unions,
- employee organisations,
- investor groups,
- consumer groups.

In a sense the company serves all of these special interests. Successful CEOs will ensure that all these audiences understand the company and find its story compelling and sympathetic. Clearly this is no easy task when some of these groups can be seen as natural antagonists.

Both investors and employees, for example, want first call over the company's profits. Should annual profits be distributed as dividends to shareholders or in profit-sharing bonuses to employees? A supplier might favour low-cost manufacturing which has an adverse environmental impact, but the public living close to the factory will take a different view.

The best companies manage themselves on the principle of enlightened self-interest. Businesses must accept that all stakeholders do have a legitimate claim on the company but must never lose sight of where their principal loyalties lie — with their owners.

SHAREHOLDERS OR STAFF? THE KNIGHT RIDDER DILEMMA

Knight Ridder is one of the best known newspaper publishing groups in the USA. It was formed from the merger of Knight Newspapers, which was famous for its big editorial budgets and Pulitzer Prize-winning journalism, and Ridder Publications, which was renowned for cost control and bottom-line focus.

A feature article in *Fortune* magazine under the title 'Tony Ridder just can't win' contains a fascinating example of the problem of serving diverse stakeholder interests. As a fully listed public company Knight Ridder had to try to meet Wall Street expectations of rising earnings. However, as with any newspaper business, its biggest cost was labour and in a soft advertising market the CEO (Tony Ridder) looked to reduce headcount. As *Fortune* commented: 'Journalists hate that he's cutting costs. Wall Street thinks he's coddling journalists.'[3]

There was very public criticism of the CEO by his own editorial staff. This included an e-mail from a reporter who had been fired which was reproduced by the *New York Times* and the *Washington Post*. It read:

> You corporate hacks take a break from your golf game
> long enough to scream that circulation must stay up, but
> then you order arbitrary budget cuts ... And when that's
> not enough, you order layoffs that eliminate the very
> employees who have helped keep circulation from falling.
> What kind of witless dolt are you? Seriously, the kid who

changes the oil in my car could run Knight Ridder with
more foresight than you.

The problem for Tony Ridder, as with any other CEO, is how to please
all your stakeholders when they have different objectives. Employees
want their jobs – indeed want pay rises and better conditions. Investors
want growing profits which, when sales are down, can only come from
cost cuts. As *Fortune* commented: 'Labor is a newspaper's biggest cost.
It's a formula any publicly owned newspaper company CEO has to accept. If he makes his numbers, he's got newsrooms full of enemies. If he
doesn't, there's hell to pay on Wall Street.'

THE UNILEVER PERSPECTIVE

The Anglo-Dutch company Unilever is one of the world's largest con-
sumer-goods companies and owns a host of famous brands. In an article
on the impact of the internet on brands, CEO Niall FitzGerald commented:

> Today, companies have nowhere to hide. Employees,
> consumers, government, suppliers, shareholders and the
> media not only take an increasing interest in every aspect
> of a company's activities, they also have the means at their
> fingertips to find out everything about them.
>   This has important implications for brand management.
> With the reputation of the entire corporation increasingly
> impinging on the reputation of each and every brand –
> and vice versa – the responsibility for the management of
> brand reputation lies at least as heavily with the chief
> executive as it does with the company's brand managers.[4]

One of the tasks of the CEO is to ensure that all the company's managers and employees recognise that any failings, even with a single brand or customer, can have a negative impact on the whole corporation.

Customers come first

Customers are a company's most important constituency, but one absent from most literature and discussions on corporate governance. It's almost as if customers are dismissed as a given.

Many failed businesses made the error of being too inward looking and too production focused. Success only really comes from making things that people want to buy, not by making things because you can. The science and art of marketing, as opposed to sales, is devoted to the formulation and reformulation of products and services that meet a real demand. The companies with the highest margins are often those that have the best feel for what the customer regards as a high-value product.

The recent obsession with shareholder value has tended to overlook the obvious. Unless a business creates value for its customers, then there is no wealth to spread around.

A virtuous circle

A company cannot simply focus on any single group of stakeholders at the expense of the others. Although the main objective must be to reward shareholders, having a broader perspective and also satisfying other groups will, ultimately, be in the shareholders' best interests.

In his book *The Mind of the CEO* Jeffrey Garten interviewed thirty chief executives. The four quotes below all come from his interviews:[5]

> People want their company to be a good citizen. They
> want it to show true concern for the world, for the
> environment. They want it to have a social conscience.
> There is now a very clear expectation – which is

coming from political life as well as our own employees
– that companies will have to have a soul. (Jorma
Ollila, chief executive of Nokia)

Companies that we trust have a huge competitive
advantage. It has become in a company's commercial
interest to be seen as a good citizen. (Sir Martin
Sorrell, chief executive of the international marketing
services group WPP)

We have done surveys of our customers which
indicate that people like to buy from companies which
they feel comfortable with. Frankly, they like to deal
with companies they wouldn't mind their friends
seeing them buy from. (Sir Mark Moody-Stuart,
chairman of Royal Dutch Shell)

I know some people assume our interest lies solely
in the maximisation of short-term profit. I am a great
believer in having to deliver a highly competitive return
to our shareholders every quarter. But I see no trade-
off between the short term and the long. Companies
can only flourish when they serve their customers and
their communities and when their employees feel
valuable and productive. (Lord Browne, chief executive
of BP)

As the interests of the various stakeholders become increasingly
intertwined, companies must recognise that what might once have
been seen as philanthropic or social gestures do actually add to the
value of the enterprise. The CEO must maintain a strong sense of
how all the various stakeholders are being treated, as line managers
will be far more focused on satisfying just one or two groups.

What is 'success' for a company?

The answer depends on perspective. Different stakeholders may well take differing points of view.

In this book I make the assumption that the measure of success is increasing shareholder wealth. This follows from superior use of capital which itself normally follows profitable growth. It is the only true yardstick of success, since it allows the company to achieve the secondary goals of providing employment, developing new goods and services and making a contribution to society.

Another way of looking at this is to say that: 'Success is earning a better than average return on capital invested'. Writing in *Fortune*, columnist Geoffrey Colivn comments:

> Political journalists have a saying: ... Follow the Money. In business journalism our mantra is – or should be – follow the capital. We get seduced by technology advances, corporate politics, marketing campaigns and market share battles. They're all important but they are not how the score is kept. Business success is ultimately about earning more money than your capital costs.[6]

A company's capital consists of *debt* – which is borrowed money. And *equity*, which is money invested by shareholders. Providers of debt are rewarded by being paid interest on a regular basis. And, one day, by being paid back the original sum lent. The annual cost of debt is the interest charge. The more risky a company is felt to be, the higher the rate of interest that will be demanded by lenders. Providers of equity are rewarded by being paid dividends and by owning the firm's shares which, they hope, will grow in value. The annual cost of equity – to the company – is harder to calculate, but is more expensive than debt because shareholders are taking more risk and expect a greater return.

The so-called *cost of capital* is a mixture of the cost of debt and

Table 1.1	Return on capital employed (ROCE) of the five largest UK companies, 2000	
Company	ROCE (%)	Cost of capital (%)
Glaxo	35	7
Shell	20	8
BP	16	8
AstraZenica	31	7
Unilever	16	7

equity. For the majority of firms this cost is between about 7 and 11 per cent a year, although this varies with prevailing interest rates and the company's balance of loans and shares. Projects and investments entered into by the firm need to earn more than the cost of capital to be creating wealth. If projects and investments constantly earn less, then investors' value is being destroyed.

As an example, Table 1.1 shows return on capital employed (ROCE) of the UK's top five companies ranked by total size for the year 2000.[7] These companies just happen to be big. They do not have the highest ROCEs in the corporate world but all clearly created wealth, as their return on capital is higher than their cost of capital. As very large, stable businesses they have a low cost of capital as they are considered less risky than smaller businesses and thus can borrow more cheaply.

The ROCE for a business will vary from year to year, but the better businesses have a consistently good record. A poor return on capital over a particular period is sometimes excused by saying that the business is building a strategic position for the future which will bring high returns in the long run. However, I am very sceptical of this view and recall the words of John Maynard Keynes: 'in the long-run we are all dead'.

Quarterly reporting is almost certainly too short-sighted in terms of judging return on capital, but if a firm does not show good and consistent returns each year it is probably following a bad business model. Investors will look to support management teams and businesses that make their capital grow in value.

It is relatively easy to increase a company's return on capital quickly. You take capital out of the business, do not make any investments, and sell off assets. As long as the customers keep buying, then your invested capital will 'work harder'. In real life things do not happen this way, because products become outdated and quality drops if cash does not go back in to make improvements. In the end, sales and profits will suffer from investment cuts.

On the other hand, it is easy to grow sales by investing heavily in new equipment and new products, so gaining market share. However, if the incremental sales achieved are less profitable and thus less rewarding in terms of return on the capital, then the capital invested is being used badly and the business is overcapitalised.

The trick is to get the balance right and invest the right amount in the right things at the right time. Easier said than done, but the only true test of success.

How much is a company worth?

The value of a company is the main way of keeping score for a CEO. Is it going up? Many business biographies start with the statement that 'X created $n million of shareholder value during his or her term of office'. But did they?

The *market value* of a company can be determined by actually selling it, or it is implied by the price at which its shares trade if it is a publicly listed company. However, the *true value* is the present value of the sum of all future cash that the business will generate … if we can ever work out what this will be.

One of the drivers of the recent corporate scandals was that whilst investors were talking about *value* in terms of the paper worth of their unrealised gains on the stock market, many executives and CEOs were busy taking out their share of that value in actual cash by selling stock and in remuneration and perks based on what proved to be hugely inflated and unsustainable share prices.

Don't believe the stock market

Some people will argue that the share price of a publicly quoted company represents its true value. This is not correct. It does represent the price you will pay to buy a small block of shares on a certain day, reflecting current levels of knowledge and investor sentiment. But there is no reason to believe it is in any way an accurate indicator of what the business is really worth. The share price is simply a reflection of the current state of public opinion.

Most companies' recent share-price graphs – particularly those in the TMT (Telecom, Media, Technology) sector – resemble a cross-section through Mount Everest, with early spring 2000 as the peak. But at what point in this dramatic rise and fall was the value the real one?

Investors in TMT convinced themselves that high growth rates would last for ever and that the internet really did represent a 'new paradigm'. When the now apparently almost worthless AOL merged with the venerable (and very valuable) media giant Time Warner in January 2000, the deal had a price tag of $150 billion and AOL shareholders laid claim to the lion's share. It was mass delusion on an extraordinary scale.

Warren Buffett, one of the most successful American investors of recent years, said in the annual report of his own company, Berkshire Hathaway, 'We do not want to maximise the price at which Berkshire shares trade … we wish for them to trade in a narrow range centred at their *intrinsic* business value.'[8] The italics are mine. I would argue the intrinsic value is the sum of all the future cash flows, if it can be calculated what these will be.

Chief executives must not be deluded by their company's share price. It merits neither praise nor criticism. It's just a snapshot of sentiment.

Cash flow is what really counts

The net cash flow is the actual cash generated each year from the company's operations after meeting all its normal operating costs and necessary investments. It is not the same as the annual 'profit'. Profit is an accounting definition which is arrived at after taking into account such things as depreciation of physical assets, the theoretical charge the company incurs each year to replace its machinery and assets as they wear out. Profit is not cash.

Companies can report profits each year but actually be going bankrupt. The most typical problem is failure to collect money from customers. The 'sales' are still recorded as a contribution to profits and the unpaid debts pile up on the balance sheet as 'receivables' or 'debtors'.

The true value is the total of the actual net cash generated each year. If you assume that borrowings do not go up or down and that shareholders neither put new cash in nor take any out, net cash is what is left over at the end of each year's trading. This produces a simple mathematical formula:

$$\text{Value of businesses} = CF1 + CF2 + CF3 + CF4 \text{ etc.,}$$

where CF1 is the net cash flow from year 1, CF2 from year 2 and so on.

This leaves two unresolved issues. First, what is the value, today, of a cash flow which occurs in the future and, second, what will those future cash flows really be?

Pick a discount rate

The question of how to value today a cash flow which will arrive in the future receives huge attention in academic circles but really comes down to the simple issue of what discount rate to apply.

The discount rate is the percentage by which the value of a future cash flow is reduced to reflect the time value of money – that is lost interest income. If a company's cash flow from next year was predictable with certainty then the value of that future cash flow today is the exact amount of money that, if deposited in a bank today, would produce that cash flow next year. Thus the discount rate is the same as the interest rate, as it reflects the interest 'lost' by not having the cash in the bank now.

In practice company cash flows are not predictable. The risk and uncertainty is reflected by using a discount rate that is a bit higher than bank interest rate. The more unpredictable the future cash flow might be, the bigger the 'bit' over and above bank interest rate has to be to reflect the uncertainty.

An entire science has grown up around the concept of the *beta*, which is a measure of the volatility of a company's share price and thus, in theory, of the unpredictability of future cash flows. But the real issue in comparing one company's value with another is not so much what discount rate to choose but in making an accurate assessment of whether future cash flows are growing or not and, if so, how quickly.

Growth is what really matters

The one thing that truly makes one company more valuable than another is its ability to grow its cash flows into the future. It does not matter how much effort is put into determining the 'right' discount rate. A fast-growing company, in terms of net cash flow, will always be worth more than a slow-growing one if they start at the same size. The reason that investors assigned what now seem ludicrous values to internet companies was not that they had a desire to waste their money but the honest belief that the growth potential of these businesses was nearly unlimited.

Growth in cash flow comes when sales are growing, either because the company gains market share and/or because it is in a market which itself is growing fast. Computers, mobile telephones, video games and health care were all fast growth markets as they reflected changes in technology and in society. Farm equipment, steel manufacturing and car production have much lower growth, for obvious reasons.

As a simple test, if a company has shown a few years of growth in an industry that seems itself to have growth prospects, investors will nearly always view it as 'growth stock' and expect its future cash flows to increase. This means they will assign it a higher value expressed in terms of a multiple of its current cash flow than a low-growth stock. There is no doubt that growth companies have more inherent value. The problem of the long bull market was that too many investors developed an unrealistic expectation of what future growth could be.

A business, then, is simply a machine to generate cash and the role of the CEO is to find ways to make that machine as efficient as possible.

2   What is a CEO?

*The performance of the CEO makes a huge difference to
companies, as is evidenced by failures in growing industries and
successes in declining ones. The great CEOs can see the wood
for the trees and are able to think of their large complex firms
in the simple language of the corner shop. The role and style of
the CEO has evolved reflecting eras in the stock market from
founder-owners through administrators to the rock stars of
recent years. Following recent failures investors are now seeking
a new breed of more balanced corporate leaders.*

The CEO plays a unique part in making a company a success or
failure. Their actions have implications for everyone in the business, for those who trade with it and those who own it.

CEOs provide leadership and direction. They set the guidelines
within which an organisation functions. They are the ones with the
responsibility for describing the vision, setting strategy, deciding the
organisation's structure, picking the people, initiating change, doing
deals and controlling communication.

A successful business is a group effort but the person in charge
carries a particular responsibility to provide purpose, energy and
motivation. A good CEO selects strong people and builds them into
a close team to achieve superior performance. A poor CEO attracts
less effective people and often does not coach them well. This produces an uncoordinated group of individuals and will result in relative failure.

Even the largest company is made up of small businesses – or
should be. A strong leader selects and encourages other strong leaders so all the business units thrive. The best large businesses consist

of many successful, small enterprises each led by highly effective, self-confident, entrepreneurial individuals. They are CEOs in spirit if not in title.

Businesses are not democracies where each decision is put to the vote. For practical reasons shareholders hand down — and, indeed, line managers hand up — disproportionate power to the CEO in order to get things done. It's the same reason that elected governments and people give so much power to presidents or prime ministers. It is the best way to get decisions made and to get a large number of people going in the same direction. However, it does put a lot of control into one person's hands.

Good CEOs have a major impact because they occupy a crucial and central organisational role which allows them to use and direct their companies' resources for specific goals. However, if these appointed leaders do their tasks badly, and if they fail to establish a clear vision and strategy, then they can be a huge impediment to change and are likely to create a dysfunctional management team. Bad CEOs destroy shareholder wealth like no other commercial force because their position carries so much power.

Do chief executives really make any difference?

There is no dispute that some companies succeed and others fail. Even within an industry there are winners and losers. Southwest, Ryanair and Jet Blue are profitable low-cost airline operators who did well in the slump following the 2001 terrorist attacks in America. British Airways, American Airways and United Airlines had an awful financial record in the same period. In what has been the very fast-growing industry of personal computers Dell has been a huge creator of wealth. Compaq and Hewlett-Packard, two of its key rivals, were a disappointment.

An individual company goes through good and bad periods. Technology giant IBM dominated the office equipment market, then reported record-breaking losses, then was re-invented. It was once great, then weak, then great again. It was a similar story with Britain's leading retailer Marks & Spencer, which went from hero to villain to hero. Although it is hard to prove, it must surely be the case that management in general and chief executives in particular do make a big difference to company performance. Lou Gerstner is felt to have rescued IBM. Roger Holmes was the revivalist leader at Marks & Spencer. Both placed great emphasis on recruiting new teams.

Every dog ...
The English writer Charles Kingsley used the phrase 'and every dog shall have his day' in 1863. And so it is with companies. All businesses have good times and bad times. People and organisations have periods of victory and defeat. The most successful CEOs do the right thing when a business is both up and down. Just being good at managing growth or having the toughness to make cost cuts is not enough. CEOs cannot be one-dimensional.

Some of the most valuable work done by good CEOs has been during periods when their company is doing badly. The success was in ensuring it did less badly than its competitors and that it was building the base for future prosperity. CEOs who do well in boom years have not been fully tested. Riding a rising tide is easy. Doing well in a slump is a better indicator. The real measure of a CEO is if their company outperforms its peers no matter what is happening in the overall economy.

In particular, CEOs are responsible for picking and motivating their managers. In an article about what it takes to succeed in a recession, *The Economist* commented: 'At times of crisis, having the right people in the right place is vital. In a boom there is enough fat to absorb some bad judgement; in a recession good management becomes a survival issue.'[1]

Is it all about risk taking?

Running a company is not about placing bets and hoping for the best. Even for the most risk-taking entrepreneurs it's a slow and meticulous process of getting lots of little things right. The commercial market place does not operate like Las Vegas. The American politician (and successful businessman) Benjamin Franklin wrote in 1735: 'Human felicity is produced not so much by great pieces of good fortune that seldom happen as much as by little advantages that occur everyday.'[2]

There is no reliable get-rich-quick answer in business – although the financial engineers and investment bankers might have it otherwise. There do appear to be moments of glittering, almost immediate, wealth creation but most of these can be seen afterwards to have been illusory paper fortunes based on flawed expectations of the future.

Success is a matter of an inspiring vision made real by an intelligent and appropriate strategy, executed well with quick and clever tactics. Formulating that strategy takes time. Making a business profitable means the CEO finding and using those 'little advantages that occur every day'.

Leadership is in the job specification

Leadership is clearly something that CEOs must do, but it is very hard to define exactly what it is. Being the chief executive means demonstrating a set of behaviours and standards which promote confidence both inside and outside the company. Commenting on leadership, the editor of *Red Herring* magazine Jason Pontin wrote in 2002:

> The best business leaders are ... modest in their lives
> and restrained in their expressions of self-importance.
> They are childishly excited by their products and
> believe the excellence of those products is the best

guarantee of success. They hope to delight and surprise
their customers. They would never lie to their
investors. Most importantly they believe their greatest
asset is the people at their companies.[3]

Although CEOs should consult widely on decisions, they are not
there to perform as politicians or to run committees to obtain consensus. They are there to act and to take decisions, having accumu-
lated all the facts and opinions.

The US Secretary of Defense during the 'War on Terrorism',
Donald Rumsfeld, was quoted as saying, 'If everyone waited until
everyone agreed on everything before one did anything, there
wouldn't be any such thing as leadership.'[4] That is good guidance for
an effective CEO.

Nature, nurture or night-school?

Only a very small percentage of business people will be appointed as
chief executives. Does the selection process ensure the most able always get the top job? Clearly it does not. Many CEOs are found to be
useless, a few even to be criminal. So what makes a good CEO? Is it
underlying features of character, a privileged educational background
or just hard work?

There is much debate as to whether political and military leaders
are born or trained. Of all unlikely people it was King Louis XVIII of
France who said to army cadets in 1819, 'Remember that there is
not one of you who does not carry in his cartridge-pouch the field
marshal's baton. It is up to you to bring it forth.'[5]

Frederick Taylor, often described as the father of modern management thinking, wrote his *Principles of Scientific Management* in 1911.
He said:

In the past the prevailing idea has been well expressed
in the saying 'Captains of industry are born, not made'.

In the future it will be appreciated that our leaders
must be trained right as well as born right. In the past
the man has been first; in the future the system will be
first.[6]

The abilities that make a good CEO are certainly present in many
business people. Getting the top job is often a matter of luck and timing. Whilst I would not go so far as Taylor in arguing that it is all down
to technique, I do believe that doing the job well is a matter of following certain principles, which I have tried to outline later in this book.

Chief executives do not have the luxury of being able to follow orders and being told what to do. They have to think about their businesses, plan for the future and decide how the business should
function. CEOs have to find the answers for themselves.

CEOs must keep it simple

Many businesses have become very complex, of great size with large
numbers of employees and international dimensions. But, even in
this environment, the best CEOs do not lose sight of the essential,
simple, truth that there are basic, fundamental, business principles
that apply equally well to the market stall or the multinational.

The long-serving British prime minister Margaret Thatcher was
said to compare running the British economy to running a corner
shop (she was a shopkeeper's daughter from a small town in Lin-
colnshire). The analogy may not have been wholly valid for a national
economy. But it does hold true for a business.

The task of the CEO is to take a simple view of a complex organisation. To see it – no matter how large or international – in the same
terms that Alderman Alfred Roberts (Mrs Thatcher's father) probably saw his grocer's shop in Grantham.

Many senior executives, running major divisions of large corporations, exhibit a lack of basic, corner-shop business sense. They

frequently have clarity about their own area of responsibility – marketing, sales, operations, production, finance – but seem unable or unwilling to grasp the overall concept. They often miss the underlying truth that the whole business only exists to create something that customers really want, and through that to make profits.

Excellence, indeed perfection, in their specific area is the corporate mission of senior people, but if they want to become CEO, or at least understand what their CEO is trying to achieve, they have to be able to break out of narrow and deep thinking and see the bigger picture:

- Sales people will pump up transaction volumes by finding new customers oblivious to the fact that poor cash collection means the business is running out of money.
- Production teams will shave pennies off the cost of an item, not realising that they are substantially reducing the product's actual or perceived quality and thus reducing margins.
- Operations managers will change procedures to simplify internal administration and to reduce costs, not knowing they are upsetting customers by making orders more complex or delayed.
- Financial controllers will introduce tough new reporting measures that appear to reduce risk and give more accurate figures but they cost far more to administer than they save in terms of cash.

Large businesses are composed of specialists who get locked into their own special issues and can lose sight of what their overall business is for. A high degree of specialisation and narrow focus – sometimes called a 'silo' mentality – can make a company very dysfunctional.

The basics of business are obvious to the successful corner-shop manager and should equally be obvious to the CEO of a multi-billion dollar multinational. Good CEOs fight, successfully, to overcome management myopia or tunnel vision. Good CEOs *do* see the wood for the trees and are able to reduce the complex to the simple. They constantly seek out and understand the external view. They understand how their customers and shareholders see the business.

CEOs are paid to think about possibilities as much as to take actions. Good leaders ask themselves lots of questions. But having fixed upon a course of action, they must be consistent. CEOs who fail are the ones who frequently change their minds or do not put the right thoughts into actions. CEOs must be hugely curious about where their business came from, what is happening elsewhere, what their competitors are doing, what their customers want and where their industry is going.

CEO: a risky job

A marked feature of business is the rapid turnover of CEOs. And it is getting faster. In November 2001 the London *Evening Standard* ran the headline 'Bloodbath in the Boardroom Puts Pressure on Chiefs', noting that the average tenure of CEOs in the USA was five and a half years and in the UK five years. John Challenger of the placement firm Challenger, Grey & Christmas was quoted:

> The CEO job has become like that of the US President. You get one term and, if you are very lucky, you get two. The board of directors is no longer a group of allies handpicked by the CEO but independent, like Congress. There is more oversight, more interference and much more questioning of what the CEO is doing.[7]

A study by consultants Booz Allen & Hamilton shows that the average tenure of CEOs in the world's 2,500 most valuable companies was 9.5 years in 1995 but down to 7.3 years by 2001.[8] A different study by the same firm showed that 39 per cent of top company

CEOs who left office in 2002 were forced out. David Newkirk of Booz Allen commented:

> Business leaders are enduring scrutiny and pressure unseen since the Great Depression. The CEO mystique has all but evaporated.[9]

By May 2002, after the market collapse, *The Business* was reporting that

> the shelf life of the modern CEO is as short as 2 years. Boards are losing patience with their CEOs. There has been too much bad news for too long. CEOs are under the microscope for many reasons, not just headline-making scandals.[10]

The conventional reason given for the increasingly shorter tenure of CEOs is that the stock market is short term in outlook and that jumpy investors force CEOs out. But it has more to do with the fact that company boards recognise that removing a failing CEO can make a real, immediate difference.

The opportunity cost of having a bad CEO in place is huge. The company may lack a well-articulated vision, which leaves employees disheartened. The lack of a defined vision results in an incoherent strategy which means the company makes bad use of resources. Lack of confidence in a leader undermines the self-confidence of managers, who then make tactical errors. Good people become disenchanted and leave. The share price falls, debt service charges rise and investors get worried. Much of the blame for all this can in many cases be laid at the door of one man or woman. Ineffective CEOs do need to be fired.

Good CEOs, on the other hand, are characteristically surrounded by good people. You cannot run a large business by yourself. Good

CEOs take the right actions but a major part of what makes them good means they share the glory and rewards with others.

CEOs infamous for dominating their business and bullying staff, or with an obvious thirst for self-publicity, are usually not very good at delivering shareholder wealth. In orchestral terms, you need a talented conductor rather than a gifted soloist in the corner office.

CEOs must outperform

Wealth for shareholders is most typically reflected by the share price of a quoted company. This price results partly from the performance of the business – its ability to make profits – and partly from perception – the expectations of how well the business will do in the future. The job of the CEO and the management team is to succeed in both areas. They must drive both annual cash flow and create confidence in future cash flows.

Some sectors of industry have far more inherent growth than do others. But this potential is visible both inside and outside the industry and tends to generate aggressive competition. High growth potential in an industry does not always mean high profits or a high stock market rating for a company. That depends on the level of competition.

Other industries have a doubtful future, obvious over-capacity and low margins. However, a good management team can make profits even in these industries and there may be the opportunity to buy weak competitors to consolidate them and achieve high investment returns. There are wealth creators even in mature industries.

CEOs who complain that their shares are undervalued probably have only themselves to blame. Either they have not been delivering growing profits and/or they have failed to convince potential investors that their company has a bright future. Whichever the cause, it is within a CEO's power to fix the problem. Profitable operation and a high rating are not simply a function of which industry sector

Table 2.1   **The world's leading wealth creators in 2001**

Rank	Company	Wealth added ($ billion)
1	Wal-Mart	150
2	Microsoft	94
3	IBM	93
4	General Electric	92
5	Citigroup	83
6	Nokia	82
7	Home Depot	59
8	Johnson & Johnson	56
9	Dell Computer	35
10	Nestlé	35

a company is in. They depend on how well the CEO does his or her job.

It is about superior returns

As explained in Chapter 1, a company succeeds when it grows in value over the years faster than the average investment. The company achieves this by getting a better return on the capital it invests than its rivals. Table 2.1 shows the world's five leading corporate creators of wealth in 2001. It is based on the work of the consulting firm Stern Stewart, who have come up with the intriguing idea of 'Wealth Added Index' (WAI).[11]

In simple terms 'wealth added' means the value created for shareholders expressed as the total returns to them (share price rise and dividends) over a five-year period. This is the dollar amount *over and above* the normal returns they would expect from an equity investment. (Of course, there are many smaller companies that have produced much better returns for shareholders in relative terms than the leviathans listed in the table, but they would come further down the list as it is ranked in terms of the volume of wealth created, not as a percentage increase.)

Any company that cannot produce returns for shareholders greater than the normal cost of equity must be considered a relative failure. Those that outperform are a success

Changing CEO styles

If CEOs did not exist we would have to invent them. All political and business systems have some concept of a 'top dog'. Every business has always needed someone in the role of leader and ultimate decision maker, but the way in which that job is done and the nature of the people who do it have changed greatly over time.

There are lots of different ways to lead a country – think of Gandhi, Mandela, Lincoln, Thatcher and Bush. The styles of corporate leadership are just as varied.

The twentieth century witnessed a transition from hard driving founder/owners to bureaucratic administrators to deal-making empire builders. In recent years we have seen the rise and fall of the 'imperial CEO' and the CEO as 'superstar'. The title 'chief executive officer' is a relatively new one, its acronym becoming widespread only in the 1980s. Before that, the leader of a business was more usually a chairman or a president or a managing director.

Figure 2.1 suggests four eras of CEO style.

Founder/owners: pre-1920

Before 1920, most companies started life as a family business where father was the boss. Many were built around an invention or a vision; many were built by one man acting on a personal mission. Henry Ford, Walt Disney, Thomas Edison. John D. Rockefeller and Alexander Graham Bell all founded companies which are still around today.

In the early days these leaders put their names over the door, owned all the shares and called all the shots. When their businesses

Figure 2.1   **The evolution of the CEO**

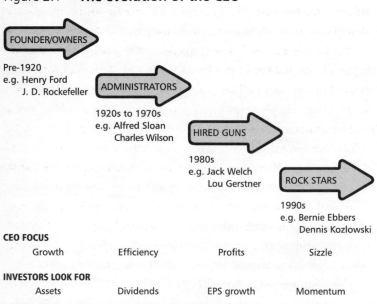

CEO FOCUS			
Growth	Efficiency	Profits	Sizzle

INVESTORS LOOK FOR			
Assets	Dividends	EPS growth	Momentum

grew and needed capital, they borrowed money, sold shares to friends and later to private investors and other companies and later still to investment institutions.

Even with outside investors the founder or his heirs often still dominated events. It was relatively rare for them to call themselves chief executives, but that is what they were. As presidents and chairmen they made business decisions to increase the value of their shares. Their personal wealth was directly linked to the value of the business. The alignment of interest between shareholder and 'CEO' was almost perfect: they were the same person.

Administrators: 1920s to 1970s

As the founding families lost interest or ran out of suitable children they needed to find professional managers. Unlike today's CEOs many of these professional administrators were simply paid a salary, albeit often a very generous one, for looking after the day-to-day affairs of the business. The founder and other larger shareholders set strategy and took key investment decisions.

The idea of the professional manager, the salaried administrator, began to take hold after the First World War. Many ran huge businesses but were not well known as individuals. Their objective often seemed to be simply to get big. The emphasis was on sales and scale.

The administrators were far more concerned with business efficiency and profit improvement rather than value creation in the modern sense. Often they faced relatively little competition and focused on building business systems rather than driving share prices.

Typical of these was Alfred Sloan who wrote *My Years with General Motors*, one of the defining business books (and allegedly Bill Gates's favourite read). Sloan pretty much invented the idea of a company split into divisions owned and controlled by a small head office.[12]

The alignment with shareholders was good as, for the most part, they wanted dividends and security and the administrators delivered this. After the Second World War, however, many big corporations started to get heavy with layers of management and the suspicion grew that senior executives looked after themselves with feather-bedded expense accounts and corporate perks while shareholders were getting a raw deal.

The stage was set for a more active management approach.

Hired guns: 1980s

As institutional shareholders and professional investors became more sophisticated and demanding, the notion of shareholder value took hold. Companies began to be run in a far more aggressive fashion. Shareholders wanted to see earnings and share prices grow. Business was under far more pressure to create value. The hostile takeover and the leveraged buyout entered the language as ways of removing underperforming complacent managers.

Leaders such as Harold Geneen, who created the conglomerate

ITT, and Jack Welch, who built General Electric, made extensive use of the tools of merger and acquisition. Business leaders were expected to be radical and tough.

The concept of 'shareholder value' started to generate much public discussion in the early 1980s and was given a big boost by the book *Creating Shareholder Value*, written by Professor Alfred Rappaport.[13] The idea of share options as a way of aligning the interests of shareholders and managers also got going in a big way in the 1980s.

The CEOs who succeeded under these conditions got rich on options, unlike many of their predecessors who relied more on salaries. But they were still, essentially, professional managers whose skill lay in building great businesses. If the stock market rose by 5 per cent a year and the star companies rose by 10 per cent a year, the options became valuable and the manager became justly wealthy.

The alignment of CEOs and shareholders seemed close as both were focused on increasing the long-term value of the business reflected by the share price. However, with the advent of the 1990s long bull market, that was about to change.

Rock stars: 1990s

As stock markets kept booming, things started getting out of hand. When overall share prices went up year after year by double digits, people with large numbers of options started to make obscene amounts of money simply as a reward for just turning up. Even a below-average performance would produce a bonanza of option gains.

Even more worrying was that investors purchased shares not because of a deep understanding of an industry that led them to believe that a company was going to grow, but simply in the belief that the share price was going to keep rising because people liked the company's 'story'. Momentum investing was born. Companies and investors became more obsessed with news flow than with cash flow.

The legendary investor Warren Buffett, who sat out the dot.com dance, was widely criticised for his conservatism. For a few years his company lost value compared with the stock market as a whole. In the UK, veteran fund manager Tony Dye also refused to follow market sentiment and was forced out of running his investment fund for short-term underperformance. Both are now enjoying hero status.

But, by and large, the entire investment industry thrived on the boom. And the new breed of CEOs was at the heart of it. For example Bernie Ebbers built WorldCom after the takeover of a small telecoms company in 1995. According to *The Economist*,

> Mr Ebbers embarked on an acquisition spree. Within a few years, he had gobbled up more than 75 companies to become a brand-new telecoms giant. Such a fervour of corporate takeovers invariably breeds adulation. The bankers and brokers all puff up their champion: the bigger his reputation, the higher his share price, the greater his buying power and the more luscious their eventual fees.[14]

The rise to prominence of the sell-side analysts – the stock pickers – who were in some ways specialist journalists, and the huge growth in the investment banking industry created a lust for deals. The bankers needed deals and the analysts needed heroes. They looked for charismatic, larger-than-life CEOs who were felt to add sizzle to a share price.

And when investors started to believe that CEOs as individuals could have a huge and immediate influence on the share price, then the era of the CEO as superstar came into its own. On the day that Michael Armstrong was announced as CEO of AT&T the market value went up by $3.8 billion and on the day that George Fisher was announced at Kodak its value leapt by $ 1.4 billion. *Fortune* magazine looked at its own role in the star CEO phenomenon and reported: 'During the 1970s it's stunning to realise how infrequently we put CEOs on the cover. Only eight times during the entire 1970s.'[15]

This changed dramatically during the 1980s and 90s. The magazine noted that since 1986 it had put Bill Gates on the cover no fewer than twenty-five times and Jack Welch thirteen times:

> Today CEOs are at the centre of our approach to
> business journalism. We know it's not perfect; for
> better or worse we've done our part to turn CEOs into
> celebrities.[16]

The Economist commented on the amount of publicity given to CEOs and the number of specialist media, which profiled them:

> There were new television channels devoted to business
> and new business magazines 'Mugs (meaning profiles)
> sell mags' is a tenet of cover designers … One piece of
> research actually found a correlation between the
> number of times that chief executives appeared on
> magazine covers and the excessive amount they had
> paid for their acquisitions. Call it the cost of hubris.[17]

The impression was given that corporate success was all down to one man or, very occasionally, woman. The era of CEO as rock star had arrived. *The Economist* explained:

> The cult of the all-powerful chief executive was
> fostered by the fact that investors found themselves lost
> in the maths of e-business. Company accounts, once a
> trusty guide, were ill equipped to measure the strange
> things going on in the new economy. Investors reverted
> to familiar faces and seductive speeches. In their search
> for winners, it was easier to follow the jockeys than the
> form.[18]

The problem got worse when CEOs started to believe their own publicity. An icon of the hard-driving 1980s was the character Gordon Gekko in the film *Wall Street*. Gekko immortalised the idea that 'greed is good', but at least it was greed based on ruthless cost cutting and actual corporate management. The fictional Gordon was a saint compared with the real-life figures that were to come after him. At least he created value for his shareholders rather than bankrupting them or spending their corporate money on $15,000 dog-shaped umbrella stands.

In the fantasy world of Gordon, 'Lunch was for wimps'. In the equally fantastic but all-too-real world of Dennis Kozlowski, lunch was paid for by the company. As were the private jet and limo that got him there.

CEOs became fabulously rich not through making great profits but by having a great story. Momentum investing meant that perceptions of *future* value became more important than actual performance. Ramping the share price by pumping quarterly earnings to drive the option value became, for many CEOs, the *only* objective. Long-term value was ignored; social responsibility and commercial integrity were denigrated. Success was measured not in terms of being well paid but in making *hundreds* of millions of dollars of capital gains.

Fallen angels: what next?

The image of the CEO as heroic corporate titan has taken a substantial hit. CEOs have been seen on national television doing the 'perp walk' arraigned in handcuffs and prison uniforms as they stand accused of a wide range of corporate crimes as well as excess and hubris. The newspapers enjoyed themselves. *The Economist*, for one:

> Fallen idols. The world is falling out of love with
> celebrity chief executives. Business leaders are being
> knocked off their pedestals faster than Communist
> heroes after the fall of the Berlin Wall.[19]

And the *Financial Times*:

> The business mighty are now fallen. The cult of the
> heroic chief executive has been ended by recession.[20]

Jeff Randall, the business editor of the BBC, writing in Britain's
Sunday Telegraph in a colourful observation said:

> The big question is: what motivated Kozlowski to
> squander shareholders' money in such a cavalier
> fashion? Why risk your career on accumulating vulgar
> and unnecessary crap? For a bullnecked barbarian who
> would not have been favourite to tell a Canaletto from a
> cannelloni, it's sadly ironic that a crude desire to
> impress New York's glitterati with conspicuous
> consumption looks like sealing his demise.[21]

On the great yardstick of the boom, 'EBITDA', Warren Buffett
commented 'References to EBITDA – Earnings Before Taxes, Depreciation and Amortization – make us shudder. It makes sense only
if you think capital expenditures are funded by the tooth fairy.'[22] In
hindsight some cynics now refer to the famous acronym as 'Earnings
Before I Tricked the Dumb Auditor'.

Momentum investing has hit a wall. EBITDA is in disgrace. Audit reports are suspect. Sustainable growth in free cash flow combined with
long-term strategic goals and social responsibility are the new orders.
The new style is about balance, consistency and action management.

The president of Sony North America, Sir Howard Stringer, commented after the boom in 2002:

> The biggest sea change is that the acquisition driven
> CEO is being replaced by the operating CEO. Deals are
> now a distraction to running the business.

The stock market slump, the dot.com implosion and various accounting scandals have taken the reputation of CEOs to an all-time low. But we cannot abolish the post. Someone has to lead companies. What sort of person, though? CEOs cannot just be administrators or their businesses will decline in the face of competition and change. But equally they must be more than gung-ho mergers and acquisitions experts and financial engineers. Being a brilliant strategist is desirable, but this must be combined with flawless execution.

Part II analyses the demands on a CEO and describes the ten tasks that define this leadership role. Success in these ten areas will ensure that their company is not just an organisation, but worthy of the description 'Enterprise'.

PART II

THE ROLE OF THE CEO

As the stock market dominoes have tumbled following the biggest equities boom in history, something significant has happened to the way we as employees, investors and customers see the role of CEOs and other senior corporate executives.

It is as if a huge wave, which had been building since the 1960s, has risen to its crest and crashed and broken. As the water swirls around we have all been left wondering what happens now. Things may look very different in the corporate world, but the philosophy behind the role of the CEO has not changed. At the start of this extraordinary period, ideas about the CEO were clear. In 1960 Professor Ted Levitt wrote:

> The organisation must learn to think of itself not as
> producing goods or services but as doing things that
> will make people want to do business with it. And the
> chief executive has the inescapable responsibility for
> creating this environment, this viewpoint, this attitude,
> this aspiration. He himself must set the company's
> style, its direction and its goals.[1]

At about the same time Alfred Sloan, the legendary boss of General Motors, observed:

> When I occupied the position of chief executive officer
> I simply exercised that power with discretion; I got
> better results by selling my ideas than by telling people
> what to do.[2]

After more than forty turbulent years, the basic ideas remain the same. Lou Gerstner of IBM wrote in 2002:

> Great institutions are not managed; they are led. They
> are not administered; they are driven by individuals

who are passionate about winning. Great CEOs roll up
their sleeves and tackle problems personally. They don't
hide behind staff. They never simply preside over the
work of others. They are visible every day with
customers, suppliers and business partners.[3]

These are all strong, clear and consistent messages. But how do
they translate into a job description and set of actions for the CEO?

Businesses create value for their customers through a very wide
range of activities, but most of the people who work in a business are
focused on accomplishing a narrow set of tasks requiring special
skills. Only a few people are paid to think about the whole business,
its structure and its future. The CEO in particular has to take this
'whole business' perspective. It is this holistic view, the general management challenge, that is the subject of the rest of this book.

For simplicity, I have selected ten tasks that define the CEO's role,
illustrated in Figure II.1. Part II looks at each of these ten tasks in
turn. Each is the subject of a separate chapter.

Figure II.1   **The CEO's ten tasks**

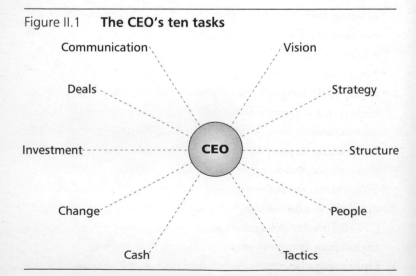

1 **Defining the business** A good road map of where a business has come from and where it is going is of value to customers and employees alike. It describes the edges of the business and its economic model. CEOs communicate a *vision* for the company but often do this by articulating existing ideas in a convincing and fresh way, rather than re-inventing the wheel.

2 **Setting clear goals** Companies must respond to competition and change by deciding how to use scarce resources to achieve their overall goals. CEOs lead the process by setting a *strategy*. The management team are part of this process and must 'buy into' the plan. Strategy evolves out of answering three questions: What is going on in our environment? How are we doing? What do we do next?

3 **Ensuring accountability** People brought together in an organisation must know what is expected of them. This means creating a *structure* for the company which defines logical business units that give managers and other employees a sense of ownership and responsibility. The CEO is the chief architect of structure, which requires political decisions.

4 **Finding talent** Getting the best *people* only starts with their recruitment. Their individual talents must be used to the full by training, coaching and through well-designed remuneration. This is mainly the task of line managers but the CEO has a role to play in devising reward systems and in managing their direct reports in a way that sets the tone for the rest of the organisation.

5 **Delegating authority** Success comes from actually getting things done. And from implementation. This means getting people throughout the business to execute well. CEOs empower managers to take the rapid day-to-day decisions. The role of the CEO is effective delegation and devolution of authority in order to put other managers in charge of *tactics*.

6 **Operating effectively** To grow in value a company must

'sweat' its assets to get the best out of them, to generate *cash*. CEOs have to ensure that all managers are focused on this. Marketing should produce maximum value for customers to drive margins; overheads have to be squeezed and capital investment kept to a minimum.

7 **Moving forward** Companies will stagnate if left to their own devices as people do not like *change*. However, the external environment and competitors do not stand still and companies must change to survive, let alone thrive. The CEO is the leading change agent in the organisation.

8 **Picking winners** Growth requires *investment* of cash. Using the right analytical tools to decide on the appropriate allocation of capital, and monitoring and managing the result, are mostly jobs for line managers. But the CEO must set the investment criteria and pick and choose among alternative uses of capital.

9 **Managing transactions** CEOs are responsible for making *deals* work. Statistics suggest that most mergers and acquisitions destroy shareholder value. A good CEO must know how to get transactions done effectively and how to manage the integration process afterwards.

10 **Telling the story** The CEO leads internal and external *communication* to produce a good image for the company, which brings benefits in more sales, improved morale and a better share price. Businesses have to actively manage their own reputation and the CEO leads that process.

These ten tasks fall to the CEO, either to lead directly as *captain* where they are the prime mover and where they must take the initiative, or to influence the outcome more indirectly as *coach*, when the task is delegated and the CEO's role is to inspire and monitor progress.

3   Defining the business: vision

*The vision for a company is a statement of why it exists and what
it is trying to achieve. Chief Executives come and go but a strong
corporate vision will survive many generations of management.
Newly appointed CEOs may decide to re-articulate the vision to
make it more relevant to current employees, investors and
customers. But it is normally better to try to find compelling new
language to express what a company is really about rather than
trying to invent a new 'big idea'. A business model underpins a
vision statement and describes how the company makes money.*

Chief executives are responsible for planning their companies'
future. To lead a business and to inspire employees requires a
clear-sighted idea of what that business is, where it came from and
where it is going.

Many people grimace at the idea that a business needs a 'vision',
considering it to be too 'Californian'. But businesses do need a clear
sense of 'why' as well as 'how', 'who' and 'what'. A well-articulated
vision gives a business meaning to shareholders, staff and customers.

The origin of the corporate vision may come from the founders of
the business or may have simply evolved over time. The current
statement of it has to come from the CEO personally, who will arrive
at it after extensive research into the business and its origins. If they
are wise they will syndicate the vision with their board of directors
and get 'buy-in' from their senior colleagues before public communication. But the personalised statement has to be theirs. CEOs who
try to be too democratic and inclusive in developing a vision – looking for one that covers all the bases and meets with everyone's
approval – will usually fail to come up with anything compelling.

CEOs are there to lead. Leaders must have followers. Followers must know where they are being taken. If the board, or senior staff, or indeed customers, no longer buy into the CEO's vision for the business then the leader is leading no longer and must be replaced. CEOs should not automatically be fired for strategic or tactical mistakes, but they must be fired for lack of vision.

The vision thing

Vision statements (particularly those crafted by consultants) often have a toe-curling, generic and hollow ring to them. Compare what you may have read in a company's annual report or handbook with this from Henry Ford:

> I will build a motorcar for the great multitude. It will be constructed of the best materials by the best men to be hired. It will be so low in price that no man making a good salary will be unable to own one and enjoy with his family the blessing of hours of pleasure in God's great open spaces. When I'm through, everybody will be able to afford one, and everyone will have one. The horse will have disappeared from our highways, the automobile will be taken for granted and we will give a large number of men employment at good wages.[1]

He said it in 1909. And apart from the bit about open spaces it remains pretty compelling today. It's the raison d'être for a company. It is a great set of reasons for owning a business, working for it and buying its products.

A vision does not have to be unique to one company. It can be, like Henry Ford's, a vision for a whole industry that will be copied by others. Neither is a vision strategy or tactics. A vision for a business gives it a reason for being and a business without a rationale will not prosper. However, vision alone is not enough to create commercial success – a viable business model and good implementation are also required.

Corporate visions that encompass the idea of being the 'world's largest' tend to have a whiff of Napoleon about them and, in any event, are almost bound to invite failure. No company can sustain the top numerical positions for ever. This is not a vision, simply an aspiration.

Equally, phrases like 'we will achieve a 15 per cent growth in earnings' are not vision statements but simply targets. They give no insight into the soul of a company, only its numerical goals. Goals and vision are not the same thing at all. A vision should inspire and have some 'wow' factor. Goals are simply marks on the pitch to record the score.

'A computer on every desk' was an articulation of vision in the early days of Microsoft by a young Bill Gates. It is simple yet broad, and hugely ambitious. The things a vision should be. And Microsoft did not even sell computers, only the software to bring them alive.

One of the key roles, possibly *the* key role, of a CEO is to tell a good story about the company they run. Employees, managers, board members, shareholders, customers and government are all more comfortable with a company if they have understood a simple and compelling story.

A vision cannot exist in a vacuum. It must address a company's history, its present position and its aspirations. It grows out of a company's origins and describes its future. Visions are not static. They can, and should, change over time – but not too much. Most of the truly great companies sustain a constant vision over many years while staying nimble on their feet with strategy and tactics.

Elements of a corporate vision

In a *Harvard Business Review* article entitled 'Building Your Company's

Vision', James Collins and Jerry Porras offer a powerful model for explaining how to articulate a corporate vision.[2] They argue it has two main elements, each of which has two sub-elements.

- Core ideology
  - core values
  - core purpose
- Envisioned future
  - audacious goal
  - vivid description

Core values are enduring features of an organisation. For example Collins and Porras say those of the Walt Disney company are 'imagination and wholesomeness'. They argue that *core purpose* is a reason that a company exists and must be something that really motivates people. For Wal-Mart they say the purpose is 'To give ordinary folk the chance to buy the same things as rich people'.

They make the point that a purely financial ambition is not inspiring: 'Maximising shareholder wealth does not inspire people at all levels of an organisation … When people in great organisations talk about their achievement, they say very little about earnings per share.'

This book argues that the main role of the CEO *is* to maximise shareholder wealth and that it is the main goal against which he or she should be judged, but I fully agree that this can be done only in an organisation which is inspired by a greater sense of purpose. Shareholder value is a by-product of a great company and cannot be an end in and of itself.

In terms of *audacious goals*, Collins and Porras's examples include Sony in the 1950s, which was 'to become the company most known for changing the worldwide poor-quality image of Japanese products'. And for a *vivid description* of a vision they use the example from Henry Ford quoted above.

'Building Your Company's Vision' is one of those seminal articles that deserves a place on every CEO's bookshelf.

THE MOUSE THAT SOLD ICE CREAM

In the early 1980s, when Disney was rescued from a financial mess by Michael Eisner, people commented on the degree to which the new team was skilled in the multi-media exploitation of the huge amount of family-entertainment material owned by the company. It was observed that Disney had come up with a 'new' vision for multi-media exploitation.

It should be remembered that when Walt Disney drew Mickey Mouse in the late 1920s the movies themselves made relatively little money and he was already thinking about merchandising. In the early 1930s Mickey's image helped sell 10 million ice-cream cones in one month and 2.5 million watches in two years.

Walt (who, incidentally, bore a passing physical resemblance to Mickey Mouse and did the original voice himself) clearly had a vision for his company to develop charming characters and then extend them into a wider commercial arena. By the late 1940s, when planning to expand his corporation's horizons, he expressed this vision for his new concept of a theme park:

> The idea of Disneyland is a simple one. It will be a place for people to find happiness and knowledge. It will be a place for parents and children to spend pleasant times in one another's company ... Here the older generation can recapture the nostalgia of days gone by and the younger generation can savour the challenge of the future.[3]

The genius of the Eisner turnaround was more a rediscovery and re-articulation of the original Disney vision rather than something new. In recent years Disney has fallen from grace in financial terms, but the core vision sustains.

RADIO WITH VISION

In 1915 radio was a technology used to send Morse signals from ships at sea and for limited long-distance point-to-point communication. David Sarnoff, who became the legendary CEO of RCA (Radio Corporation of America), was at the time a 25-year-old middle-ranking executive. He wrote in an internal memorandum:

> I have in mind a plan of development which would make the radio a household utility in the same sense as a piano or the phonograph. The idea is to bring music into the home by wireless. Baseball scores could be transmitted into the air from one set installed at the stadium and broadcast to the multitude at home.[4]

It would be nearly ten years before this vision was translated into a reality but it was the foundation for the company that was one of the fastest growing in America, and which ended up as the NBC broadcasting network, part of General Electric. They have gone on to become leaders in developing broadcast television and subsequently in the cable and internet businesses. The vision of making a technology a household utility has held good for nearly a century.

NOT VISION BUT CLEAR SIGHT

Lou Gerstner took over IBM in the spring of 1993. At the time it had just reported the then largest loss in corporate history of some $5 billion. IBM had started life as a machine maker – hence International Business Machines. It become the byword for mainframe computers 'big iron' and it pioneered the personal computer. Indeed the 'PC' started life as a specific IBM brand.

But they lost the plot. Costs escalated, new competitors took market share, divisions indulged in in-fighting and there was much talk of breaking the business up. The long-time CEO was fired and Gerstner took over. He said right at the start that he was too busy to have a vision and just wanted to get on with it:

> The last thing IBM needs right now is a vision. What IBM needs right now is a series of very tough-minded, market-driven, highly effective strategies in each of its businesses.[5]

But of course, in a way, that was an articulation of the vision. It was a rallying cry to focus on each business and to put all the emphasis on execution. It was a simple statement of intent, not an over-complex and theoretical idea.

Indeed, there is evidence that Lou Gerstner fully supported the importance of corporate vision, evidenced by this quote made in 1985 when he was CEO of American Express:

> You have first to decide what kind of company you want to have. If you don't have a vision you believe, you can't achieve it. People just won't believe you and you won't communicate it effectively in everything you do.[6]

Do we have a business model that works?

The great internet bubble produced much excitement and created and destroyed much wealth. It also resulted in a full-frontal attack on the English language (led, mostly, by New Economy evangelists from northern California). Out of the debris of lost billions of dollars and inelegant attempts to turn nouns into verbs came a new language which has left us with some useful commercial concepts.

One of the most valuable and most abused of these is the 'business model'. A simple yet powerful idea which essentially asks the question, 'How does my business concept or vision translate into profits?' It is an unfortunate irony that so many venture capitalists and would-be dot.com billionaires failed to accept that the answer was, 'It doesn't'.

A business model is not a business vision, but it underpins a vision. It shows how ideas can translate into sustainable cash flow.

But a business model is much more than a series of spreadsheets which, literally, *model* the performance of a business under various assumptions. A good business model is a coherent, simple description of why a business works. It is an engaging story that can be told in just a few words. What Hollywood producers might call 'high concept'.

Neither is a business model a strategy. A strategy describes ways of making the model work and, particularly, how to deal with competitors and changes in the environment, and is the subject of Chapter 4.

The discussion of a business model brings together the two basic questions that any CEO and management team must ask themselves:

1 Is there a demand for our product/service?
2 Can we serve that demand and make a profit?

A workable business model

By way of an example let's assume a group of us move to a small town and decide to open a restaurant that sells hamburgers, French fries and coffee. We'll buy the food in bulk from a local wholesaler and get college kids to cook it. We will try to sell it for 20 per cent more than it costs us to provide it.

There is no doubt that the demand exists. People have to eat and, unless the whole town is vegetarian, a hamburger is a staple item. No doubt also that it is possible to buy the raw materials and process them at a cost that is less than you can charge people. In essence we are offering to do for people what they could do for themselves. It's a service we can provide at a profit because it creates value for the customer.

So, the business model works because there is a demand we can meet at a cost which allows us to make a surplus.

The problem is that McDonald's might already be in the town. If so, they will almost certainly do fast food better than us, so our business may well fail unless there is more demand than McDonald's can meet, or unless we can find an 'angle'.

The business model will only continue to work if it is modified in the face of competition which may be able to meet all the demand more effectively.

A unworkable business model

However, some business models seem doomed from the start, which makes it even more of a mystery when they receive investment.

Grocery stores, for example – supermarkets and hypermarkets – already operate with very thin margins as intense competition keeps prices low and they have already squeezed the best possible terms from suppliers.

Internet-based grocery retailers faced an impossible task. Customers would not pay more for their food shopping, suppliers would not, probably could not, give better terms. Worse still, in the conventional store it is usually the customers themselves who pay to move the goods from the shop to their homes. The web-based services had to pick up all these delivery costs themselves.

Despite this, the California-based online grocer Webvan raised $275 million at its IPO in July 1999. It closed just two years later. Established retailers such as the UK's Tesco have made a success of online ordering, but only because they operate it as a bolt-on to their existing business.

Another type of online retailing that was doomed even at the planning stage was furniture sales. The web-based retailer Furniture.com was reported to have spent $2.5 million on their domain name before they sold a stick of anything. To be competitive with bricks-and-mortar retailers they had to keep their prices low but, as one ex-employee notes, 'There were many cases when we would get an order for a $200 end-table and then spend $300 to ship it.'[7]

Books and CDs are a very different matter, as Amazon is proving. Customers are happy to buy electronically, shipping costs are relatively low and the range offered online can be much greater than in any store. The model works.

TRAVELLER'S CHEQUES FROM AMERICAN EXPRESS

The story of American Express is well known. It was started in 1850 by two of the most famous names in US finance, Henry Wells and William Fargo. At first it grew by offering freight- and money-transfer services along the mushrooming railroad network.

In the 1880s Fargo's brother 'J.C.' pioneered the idea of the Traveller's Cheque to replace the old letter of credit following a trip to Europe, where he experienced first hand the problems of obtaining foreign currency. The traveller's cheque, backed by the good name of American Express, became a solution to a real problem. Tourists wanted the 'universal money' as it made their lives easier. Shops and hotels wanted to accept the cheques as it brought them more American customers.

Author Joan Magretta explained why the business model was so brilliant:

> American Express has discovered a risk-less business ... Because people always paid cash for the checks before (often long before) they used them American Express was getting an interest free loan from its customers ... Fargo's business model changed the rules of the game and the economics of travel.[8]

Identifying the 'edges' of the business

Another aspect of the definition of a business is a clear understanding of where the business starts and ends and where other companies' boundaries lie. Employees and customers need to have a feeling for what the business regards as its legitimate territory and where it stops.

The Walt Disney Company originated with animated films. It moved easily into conventional movies, television, radio and theme parks. The strong character identities it created and owned led it into toys. The theme parks opened the way to operate cruise ships, and then branded island resorts. The movies have been recycled as Broadway shows.

The true conglomerates, like ITT (hotels, insurance, food manufacture, telephony), Hanson (building products, construction, electrical goods, radio) and General Electric (anything from fridge-freezers to nuclear power stations to television broadcasting), tend to focus their visions more on *how* they operate rather than in what industry. Stock markets tend to be suspicious of conglomerates and mark down their share values, fearing they are not as operationally strong as more focused businesses and that they are prone to financial engineering to boost apparent earnings. They are businesses without a clear edge.

The aggressive extension of a brand to cover many goods and services is also questionable in terms of losing focus. For example, Virgin includes airlines, clubs, records, radio stations, soft drinks, and financial investment products. Can one brand really add value across such a wide range?

Diversification does reduce risk, but for the most part investors prefer to achieve this themselves by buying several specialist businesses rather than encouraging managers to do it for them.

Lack of definition can blur the edges of the core business. The theory is that investors prefer to put their money into 'pure plays' and will punish ill-defined businesses with a 'conglomerate discount'. It is a common cause of business failure when the edges of a business become so blurred that people lose sight of what the core business is really meant to be.

Culture

The way a company behaves and the way its people behave are often described as its culture or style. A strong culture can make implementation and decision making easier as people know what's expected of them. A weak, hard-to-identify culture is almost always linked to a lack of vision and clarity in respect of what a company is about and where it is going. Companies with a clear vision have a sense of mission and a culture develops from that.

Culture is not really part of a vision, in the sense that an articulated vision would not normally include the words 'and the culture of this company will be …'. However, there is no doubt that the culture grows out of the vision, and a company's culture and style are enormously important in determining its success.

Although difficult to express in great detail, people, both inside and outside, do recognise cultures as being real and different. Companies are described as 'aggressive', 'bureaucratic', 'hierarchical', 'paternalistic', 'entrepreneurial'. We all know what these terms mean and can easily think of various examples. Some companies are felt to have high integrity. Some not. Some make their decisions on intellectual analysis, some more on gut instinct.

Lou Gerstner, the CEO credited with successfully turning round IBM, commented:

> Until I came to IBM, I probably would have told you
> that culture was just one among several important
> elements in any organisation's make up and success …
> But I came to see in my decade at IBM, that culture
> isn't just one aspect of the game – it is the game. In the

end, an organisation is nothing more than the collective capacity of its people to create value.[9]

Ideally, a CEO comes into the job finding a culture and style that is right for the business and upon which he or she can build. If, however, a company needs to change its attitude, the CEO needs to lead this change.

IBM had to become less arrogant under Lou Gerstner. General Electric made the transition from bureaucracy to informality under Jack Welch. Saving the UK retailer Marks & Spencer required it to look outwards rather than inwards.

Changing these characteristics do not change a company's vision. Neither are they issues of structure or resources. It is simply about changing behaviour and attitude so that they are consistent with the vision.

Articulating a vision for your company

Most CEOs do not found their company. They find themselves running it. They are dropped into the top job through either internal promotion or external recruitment.

In a few, too few, cases the outgoing CEO and the board manage the transition well and the new person takes over a well-oiled machine with an effective and accepted vision already in place. However, in many cases the arrival of a new boss is probably an indication of the failure of the previous one. This means a new statement of the vision is required. In fact even in the case of the well-managed transition a new vision is usually necessary as things move on and companies need constant renewal.

An effective vision understands and interprets the past, correctly analyses the present and paints a compelling picture of the desired future. Developing or, more usually, refining and re-stating a corporate vision is a matter of asking questions:

- Where does this business originate from?
- What product or service do we actually sell?
- How does the company run?
- What are the objectives of our owners (shareholders)?
- What are the real needs/wants of our customers?
- In what ways do we intend to change our industry or, indeed, the world?
- How are we perceived at present? Is this accurate/fair?

A vision does not need to be unique to a company but it must be appealing to, and easily understood by, shareholders, employees and customers alike. For example:

- We will make shoes of such elegance and quality that the world's rich will seek us out as their supplier. They will reflect our origins as one of the oldest shoe manufacturers in Florence.
- We will offer our community the best range of quality shoes and boots at the prices our local customers can afford. Our service to customers will be as good as it was when our grandparents owned the store.
- We will produce wine of the very highest quality that will find a place on the world's most exclusive restaurant tables. Our output will be as good as anything this vineyard produced in the past 200 years.
- We will supply wine that is a good affordable everyday drink to complement people's meals at home. Using modern technology and scientific agricultural methods we will maintain quality whilst producing high volumes.

All of these statements could describe successful businesses. They are businesses that are fun to work for and make excellent returns for their owners. They recognise the past, reflect the present and set a goal for the future. They differentiate the company and mark a clear path.

Don't mess with success

Of course, appointing a new CEO for a company does not necessarily mean that a company requires a new vision. In many cases the vision is just fine and it is strategy and/or execution that needs improvement. An attempt to force unnecessary change would be damaging.

A company's governing mission and principles may have been, and may continue to be, appropriate. The challenge then is for a CEO to ensure that they articulate the vision in a way relevant to the current audience of employees, customers and shareholders.

The vision for a company should reveal a deep understanding of why it was founded, where it came from and where it is going. CEOs should be familiar with a company's origins and be curious as to why a business came to be the way it is. They should read old materials and seek to talk with long-standing and retired employees. They should become experts in 'industrial archaeology' to help them understand and interpret the past.

The British advertising leader Robin Wight uses this phrase when he takes on a new account: 'We must interrogate the brand until it confesses its strengths'. The same logic applies to a CEO taking on a new company.

The best statements of a vision – even a new vision – will always be deeply rooted in the past.

And after the vision is clear?

Without a well-understood vision it is hard to develop a sensible strategy. Nor is it easy to design a structure, put in place operational tactics, or to recruit and retain good people. All these elements of a business start from the definition of what that business is trying to be. Strategy evolves from vision and the other elements of running the business evolve from strategy as shown in Figure 3.1.

The following two cases illustrate the progression.

Figure 3.1   **The vision sets the agenda**

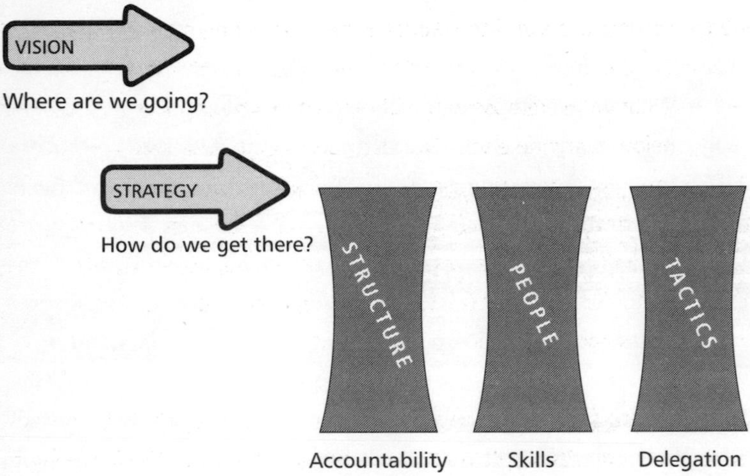

EVERYDAY LOW PRICES AT WAL-MART

Wal-Mart has grown to be the world's biggest retailer in less than fifty years. The original *vision* was to make everyday goods available to people at very low prices.

In his autobiography, Sam Walton describes the basis of his *business model*:

> Here's the simple lesson we learned which eventually
> changed the way retailers sell and customers buy all across
> America: say I bought an item for 80 cents. I found that by
> pricing it at $1.00 I could sell three times more of it than
> by pricing it at $1.20. I might make only half the profit per
> item, but because I was selling three times as many, the
> overall profit was greater. Simple enough.[10]

Volume allowed for higher profits despite lower margins. This business model was visible and available to others, of course, but Walton made it work through the *strategy* of focusing on small towns where there were no competitors and the *tactics* of an unwavering focus on costs.

> What we were obsessed with was keeping our prices below everyone else's. Our dedication to that idea was total. Everybody worked like crazy to keep the expenses down. Our stores didn't really look that good – they weren't professional at all. The idea was simple: when customers thought of Wal-Mart, they should think of low prices and satisfaction guaranteed.[11]

The consistent focus on low cost and low prices is a key part of the Wal-Mart vision. Sam Walton's book even recounts that the Wal-Mart name was preferred to Walton's Market as it had only seven letters, and was thus cheap to put up and display over storefronts.

SOMETHING FOR NOTHING FROM J.-C. DECAUX

Up until the 1960s most outdoor advertising consisted of billboards on buildings and by the side of roads, which were erected by local speculators who paid rent to local landlords. Most municipal authorities and planners disliked billboards as 'visual pollution' but put up with them.

In Lyon, France, an entrepreneur, Jean-Claude Decaux, recognised that towns and cities did not benefit from the outdoor advertising and that French authorities did not have the cash to put up enough bus shelters for the rapidly growing public transport network. He came up with the idea of providing such 'street furniture' at his cost in return for the rights to sell advertising on them.

His *vision* was municipal partnerships. The *business model* was to offer to build and maintain the bus shelters at no cost to the city in return for the right to sell the advertising.

To maintain his lead, Decaux's *strategy* was to re-invest his considerable profits in working with leading designers to create ranges of products not available to his competitors, thus creating barriers to entry. These included advertising-funded public toilets, which led to his French nickname 'Le Roi de la Sanisette'.

Now there is virtually no city in the world that does not fund its street furniture by advertising. It's a business model and strategy that make this vision real.

Summary

- A compelling vision distinguishes an 'enterprise' from a mere 'organisation'.
- CEOs must define the future of their companies by articulating a vision and describing the business model. They also set cultural standards and identify the edges of the business. They must provide their companies with a clear sense of purpose.
- A new CEO normally re-articulates the existing vision in a compelling way rather than developing a new one.
- Employees, suppliers, business partners and investors need to understand why the business exists and what it aspires to achieve.
- Based on the vision a company can develop strategy and tactics; but without an engaging vision it is unlikely to be a great performer.

4 Setting clear goals: strategy

Devising strategy is a task for the CEO to lead personally. It will develop from the corporate vision and be fashioned by changes in the market place, the behaviour of competitors and the needs of customers. Strategy is about how to make the best use of resources to achieve goals in the face of competition. It requires asking detailed questions about where the company is and where it should go in order to generate returns consistently greater than its cost of capital.

The last chapter described vision – the reason a business exists. This chapter is about strategy – how to turn that vision into profitable growth. Later chapters on structure, people and tactics concern the implementation of strategy.

To articulate the corporate vision, a CEO must have a strong feeling for where the business is going, but this is as much about emotion and experience as it is about analysis and data gathering. By contrast, developing the strategy is a more scientific task based on asking questions, getting information, analysing data and forecasting future behaviour.

An effective corporate strategy requires the collaboration of many people but is usually done by a small team – led by the CEO – which brings together the required skills and knowledge. The process involves a detailed, fact-based assessment of the market place, customers and competitors.

The strategy sets the medium-term direction for the company. It is the blueprint for best use of resources to achieve defined goals. It is the way to turn the vision into reality. It is a set of assumptions, policies or guidelines which should inform all key decisions about investment, acquisitions, disposals, hiring, firing, organic growth and so on.

A sound strategy is based on knowledge of your environment – your customers, your competitors, your suppliers and your markets. Developing an effective strategy is not just a matter of experience. Indeed, experience can sometimes be a positive disadvantage. People who have been in one company or one industry too long tend to be blind to significant external developments. Too much experience and not enough analysis can lead to complacency: 'Well, that's the way we do things around here,' or, 'We've been at this a long time, we know what's right.'

Many computer experts, bred in the mainframe world of IBM, simply refused to accept the threat posed by the personal computer in the 1980s. A near collapse of IBM followed. The experienced retailers who led the UK high-street giant Marks & Spencer turned the company into a disaster zone because they became arrogant and inward looking and did not see how consumer tastes were changing around them in the 1990s and how competitors were responding.

Even the software experts at Microsoft – who did so much to make the PC triumphant – seemed, at one time, myopic to the threat posed by the internet to their proven model of licensing software to individual users. However, evidence suggests that the Microsoft culture embodies a type of restless (and in corporate terms healthy) paranoia that made them alert to such changes and ready to respond.

Andy Grove – the founder of Intel – famously said (and entitled a book), 'Only the paranoid survive'. Good advice when it comes to strategy. Strategy boils down to lots and lots of questions and a constant concern about what is going on. Good strategists are always looking over their shoulders as well as scanning the horizon.

Why do businesses need a strategy?

The strategy is a plan to make the business model work in the face of competition and change. Taken another way, this means plotting the course to make the best use of the company's assets and to capture the benefits of new investments which have high returns.

All businesses have the potential to obtain cash (by selling shares in themselves, from bank borrowings or from profitable operations) and that cash must be re-invested in an effective way. A good strategy positions a company to make the right investments. A company without a convincing strategy will leave its owners, managers and employees feeling adrift and uncertain. It will fail to focus on profitable investments and will probably not be able to raise money, as it has no convincing investor story. Its performance will suffer and it will lose out to more determined competitors.

Even if a business is generating cash today, the lack of a strategy for the future will make it vulnerable to a hostile take over by any predator able to convince investors that it would make better use of the company's cash than the incumbent management.

Who should formulate strategy?

Unlike vision, strategy cannot be a 'one-man show'. The strategy-formulation process should be led by the CEO, but it needs many different inputs. The basic knowledge required includes:

- history of company and industry,
- customer needs,
- competitor behaviour,
- strengths and weaknesses of the company.

The role of director of strategy is one of the most abused and least well defined in a corporation. Sometimes it is a senior assistant to the CEO; at other companies it is a 'Head of development' who looks for and does deals. At others it might be akin to a research manager, processing data and producing reports. The director of strategy, if the post exists, should be the person in charge of information and analysis who uses that knowledge constantly to question the status quo and look for new opportunities.

The strategy process needs to involve many line managers and functional specialists as well as seeking input from customers and suppliers.

How is strategy developed?

Strategy is a part of the business process where professional analysts and external consultants come into their own. It requires a great deal of information and 'number crunching'. Strategy development evolves from asking three main questions:

- What is happening out there?
- How are we doing ourselves?
- Where are we going?

These three questions provide the structure for the rest of this chapter.

What is happening out there?

Strategy is about where the company *will* be and, as such, requires an attempt to predict the future. This attempt needs to be grounded in the present and will emerge from an understanding of the forces that are shaping the industry or industries in which the business operates. The context of a business starts with the overall economy and then the specific industry in which the business operates (see Figure 4.1).

The macro economy

The starting point for a company's strategy is a broad perspective on the direction of overall economy. If it looks like there will be a

Figure 4.1   **Strategy develops from context**

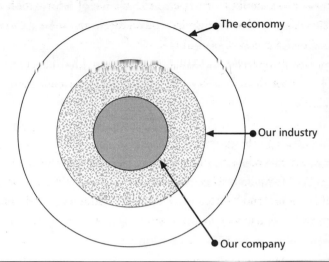

prolonged boom in consumer spending and a growth in gross domestic product, then a business will probably have a bullish approach towards new investment and expansion. The prospect of an economic slump will result in a more conservative attitude.

At the macro level (i.e. the performance of the national or international economy) the economic picture should look similar to all industries and companies. There is certainly no shortage of attempts to forecast prospects to help companies form a point of view. Institutions such as the US Federal Reserve and the Bank of England make their expectations public. Thus the impact of the broad economy should be the same on most companies, but it remains important that CEOs and their teams have an agreed understanding of how they interpret the messages about the economy to make sure they are all 'on the same page'.

Industry issues
Any individual industry may thrive or decline whatever is happening

in the overall economy. This is where changes in society and the competitive behaviour of individual firms make a difference.

Even in a growing economy, industries that have been overtaken by technical or social development will shrink. The manufacturers of buggy whips did famously badly following the invention of the auto-mobile. The operators of cross-Channel ferries between Britain and France saw an inevitable slump after the opening of the Channel Tunnel, despite the background of an economic boom. Industries manufacturing mobile phones and laptop computers will see huge sales increases even if the economy is in recession, as they are bring-ing a new technology to market.

If an industry sector has poor prospects a company may decide to try to exit from a particular business, or it might decide to become the industry consolidator and buy up many small businesses to cap-ture economies of scale. Even in declining industries strong and growing profits can be made by consolidation and cost savings.

Michael Porter's forces

Strategy formulation is one of the most covered topics in business schools and business books. It is very prone to fashion and fad. But there are some enduring basic ideas.

In my view there is one set of frameworks that has stood the test of time and which is of great value to any CEO setting up a team to formulate strategy and, in particular, to understand the dynamics of an industry.

The *Michael Porter* approach gives a robust methodology which people can easily understand and implement. It helps to ensure that the right analysis is done and is a very useful mechanism for com-municating findings to a wider management group. Figure 4.2 is adapted from Professor Porter's first major book on the subject – *Competitive Strategy* – which was published in 1980. It may be more than twenty years old but it is the simplest and most effective ap-proach I have come across.[1]

Figure 4.2   **Michael Porter's five forces**

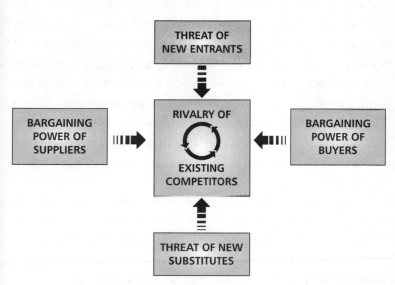

Source: Michael Porter, *Competitive Strategy*, 1980, p. 4.

The underlying idea of Professor Porter's approach is that there are five forces which act upon a company. The stronger the forces, the more power is at work driving margins downwards. A company must understand and analyse each of the five forces and predict their future intensity. If all the forces are weak the company will be highly profitable. If all the forces are strong the company will be under far more pressure. As a general rule it is more attractive and profitable to be in an environment of low competitive intensity.

In formulating strategy CEOs must ask themselves what is likely to happen to each of the five forces in the future and plot a course accordingly. The approach works so well because it requires CEOs and their teams to think about what is really going on inside and outside their business and also to ask themselves how this might all change in the future. It is an excellent framework for managing a strategy-development process as well as for analysing and presenting the results to employees and investors.

Buyers

A company's customers will have more or less power depending on their size. Rupert Murdoch's News Corporation, for example, pays far less for its newsprint than a small local newspaper owned by an independent business. If you are a food manufacturer selling to Carrefour, Wal-Mart or Tesco, you are trying to negotiate with a very powerful buyer who will, ultimately, dictate what profit margin you can make.

If there are a few large buyers, suppliers will usually be at a disadvantage.

Suppliers

If your business needs industrial diamonds you will almost certainly have to talk to De Beers. If you need computer software, which has worldwide compatibility and service you will, probably, be having a conversation with Microsoft.

If suppliers are few and far between and the customer base is fragmented, as is the case for computer software, the power is with the supplier.

New entrants

If an industry is growing and the profit margins of the firms in it are high, it will be attractive to new entrants who will believe they can get a better return on their capital by going into this new business than they can in their own current operation.

The barriers to entry into an industry are typically economies of scale and network effects. It's hard to get into mass-market car manufacturing or chemical production or oil refining unless you already have substantial production facilities. Setting up a hamburger or pizza store is easy, but it is very hard to buy the raw materials as cheaply as McDonald's can.

Strong brands are also barriers. Brewing a new beer is not hugely difficult. Persuading people to switch from Budweiser or Heineken to your new brew is much more of a problem.

Industries with low barriers include those where scale is not a key economic driver and brands are not so important, such as advertising and public relations.

Substitutes

If coffee becomes too expensive, people will drink tea. If profit margins on petrol made it very costly, people would switch to diesel. Of course the coffee to tea conversion has zero switching costs – apart perhaps from the price of a teapot – while to move from one fuel to another may require a new vehicle. Nevertheless, if the price difference is great enough, people will do it.

New technology frequently creates effective substitutes. The letter was challenged by the fax. The fax by the e-mail.

Competitors

The intensity with which firms in an industry compete is another pressure on margins. In general, competition is greatest in slow-growing industries with large numbers of equally resourced firms. Industries with high fixed costs – hotel groups, airlines, chemicals manufacturers – will also be competitive since the owners of the assets will often discount prices to try to increase their own capacity utilisation.

Intense competition can result from a number of firms having the same idea about an attractive strategic positioning and all ending up in the same place competing against each other on price. The huge overpayment by mobile telephone companies for 3G licences illustrates the danger of competitors having near-identical strategies.

How are we doing ourselves?

The analysis just described looks at what is happening in an industry and provides a picture of how that industry is likely to develop and what are the most attractive positioning options in its landscape. It is an external perspective.

Companies must also be realistic about their own strengths and weaknesses – their core competences, assets and liabilities – before they can decide which path to follow. In order to decide where you are going you must know whence you start. Companies need to be honest and introspective about themselves. There is little point in deciding on a particular strategic approach in terms of the market place if your own business is not capable of doing what is needed.

If all the evidence suggests that one ideal future positioning in an industry is that of the low-cost supplier, then a firm which already has very high, fixed operating expenses is less likely to succeed in that positioning than one which is already a low-cost operator.

If the evidence of a strategy study suggests that consumers will pay high prices for 'heritage brands' with a long history, then a business which is currently a 'no-name' manufacturer is going to find it tough to compete in that market.

If it appears that the consumer will demand ever greater choice in clothing, this is bad news for a retailer who has small stores without the merchandising space to display extensive ranges.

Realism is an important part of the process. One reason that management consultants get so much work in the strategy area is that they have the external objectivity to take an honest view of a company's strengths and weaknesses.

Benchmarking

A good place to begin self-analysis is comparative performance against industry peers:

- What has been our historic rate of sales growth?

- What are our operating margins?
- How productive are our employees?

Comparative data can come from industry trade associations, annual reports, stock market analysis and customer surveys

A particularly useful analysis is to understand exactly where profits come from within a company and then seek to focus on the most profitable areas. Typical information includes:

- profit by customer,
- profit by product,
- profit by region.

In order to get this information assumptions must sometimes be made about allocation of costs, but this is less difficult than many line managers believe.

It is amazing how many times this type of analysis will reveal a classic *Pareto principle*, also known as the 80/20 rule. Typically, only 20 per cent of the products will account for 80 per cent of the profits. In other words, a lot of the activity contributes not much to the bottom line.

The comparative positioning of a company against its competitors lies at the heart of most strategy studies. This makes use of the consultant's favourite device: the 'four box matrix'. Figure 4.3 shows the relative positioning for radio stations in a typical large city. The audience is analysed in terms of age and income (the two axes of the graph).

The various radio stations are then mapped into the four boxes in terms of the nature of their audience (as revealed by research). The larger the circle the bigger the audience in terms of number of hours spent listening to that station. This is the measure that advertisers are interested in when buying spots.

The speech station has a big audience in terms of hours listened

Figure 4.3   **The 'four-box' matrix – segmenting radio stations**

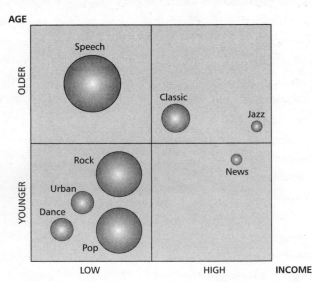

(large circle) but most of its listeners are 'older' and 'low income'. This is because a lot of home-based retirees have the time and inclination to listen to conversation. The jazz station has a much smaller audience, who also tend to be 'older' but who are 'high income'. These people like jazz but there are fewer of them in the population, and more of them seem to enjoy classical music.

The younger, lower-income groups are served, perhaps over-served, by many formats. An example of too many businesses converging on the same desirable market.

From the perspective of radio advertisers the younger, high-income audience is very attractive, but can currently only be reached by the news format. So the simple strategic conclusion from looking at the four-box chart might be there is a gap in the market for stations to reach that under-served group. But there are not that many of them in the population and they do not spend much time listening to the radio as they are busy at work. Also the news format (which does reach them) is the most expensive to produce.

Sometimes gaps in the market exist for a very good reason.

Where are we going?

The third strategic question is about direction. A clear picture of the business environment combined with an honest assessment of the company's position is the base for formulating a plan of action. It is this plan which is most commonly called the 'strategy'.

The ideal strategy is based on finding a position in an industry that allows you to charge the highest prices and to operate at the lowest costs. Another way of describing that might be to have a monopoly, which is, of course, illegal in most countries. The goal is to achieve a monopoly-like effect through strong barriers to entry, brands, proprietary technology and a unique positioning.

To say 'We have a good strategy' is not the same as 'We are very efficient at operations'. Being good at running the business is normally an important part of making a strategy successful, but it is not a strategy in and of itself.

There is little point in a retailer adopting an 'everyday low prices' or 'never knowingly undersold' approach if they actually have high costs of purchase, logistics and real estate. Equally there is little point in a retailer adopting a 'highly exclusive range' or 'high levels of personal service' approach if all their stores are out-of-town warehouses and their staff is poorly trained and on minimum wage.

Southwest and Ryanair have the strategy of being low-cost, point-to-point airlines. British Airways and Singapore Airlines are full-service carriers. Wal-Mart is a low-cost/high-volume general retailer. Gap focuses on low-cost fashionable clothes. Nieman Marcus and Harrods target affluent, price insensitive customers. All are perfectly good strategies. Success or failure is in the execution.

In my own industry – the media – a popular strategy is the

vertically integrated conglomerate. AOL Time Warner, Disney, News Corporation and Viacom all broadly fit this model. At the time of writing, the last two seem to be doing much better than the first pair. The strategies are similar but the execution is more effective.

A great strategy does not ensure success but a flawed strategy will guarantee failure.

Strategic positioning

Much of the management literature over the past twenty years has been about strategy, and much of that has been about positioning. It has described solutions about where to locate a company within an industry. Where to place it in a four-box matrix to get the best profit margins in the future. The trade-offs in positioning include:

- low cost vs high cost,
- full service vs self-service,
- broad range vs narrow range.

Defining a strategy is about making choices, but there have been many attempts to provide strategy 'ready made'.

Generic strategies: strategy in a box

It was once very fashionable in business schools to look for generic strategies. The Holy Grail was to come up with an ideal positioning for companies to aim for. The idea was to find standard answers to complex strategic issues.

One of the earliest models was probably the Boston Consulting Group's so-called growth/share matrix (see Figure 4.4), which was devised in the 1960s and was designed to help the CEOs of conglomerates decide what to do with their various divisions.

The idea was simple. A business with a high market share in a sector of the economy that had high growth was a star and thus deserved

Figure 4.4   **The growth/share matrix**

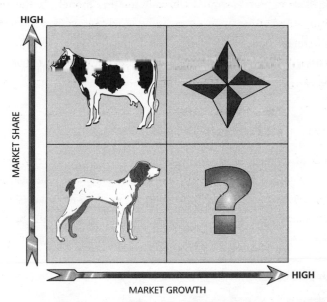

investment. A business with a low market share in a low-growth segment was a dog and should be sold off. Cash cows had high market
shares in low-growth areas and could be relied upon to generate cash
but should not have investment made into them. Question marks – low
share in a high-growth segment – had potential but carried some risks.

The implication was that once you had decided which box a business was in, then you would know what to do with it.

These ideas seem to have worked their way deep into the business
psyche. When I was a McKinsey consultant in the 1980s I was frequently confronted by managers who had analysed their own businesses along these lines. Perhaps not surprisingly, their own divisions
were normally 'stars' and those of others were 'dogs'. They often had
their own strategic answers – complete with consultants' jargon –
even before the consulting study had started.

In his original 1980s work Michael Porter identified three generic strategies:

- Cost leadership
- Differentiation
- Focus.

Some businesses tried to adopt these as 'off-the-shelf' solutions but usually failed, as they did not follow through with all the elements of execution that the strategy implied.

Many management techniques, such as total quality management, re-engineering, six sigma, quality circles and core competences, have been spoken of as generic strategies. But they are not really strategies at all. They are useful management tools which can make a business better but do not answer the key questions about environment and competitors, or provide an answer to the question, 'How do we achieve the goals inherent in the company vision?'

Businesses are just like individuals. Whilst certain approaches to overall grooming, clothes and cosmetics are better than others, everyone has their own unique combination that makes them look their best. The same is true for organisations: there is no 'one-size-fits-all' strategy. The right answer emerges from the unique circumstances of the business.

Strategy must translate into operations

A strategy will only work if it can be, and is, implemented. To decide to be a low-cost airline means doing everything consistent with this goal. Do not serve destinations for political or historic reasons, only fly where there is demand. Do not serve luxury meals – or indeed any at all. Do not pre-assign seats. Keep turnround times at gates very short and perhaps make passengers carry their own luggage.

Strategy must be consistently implemented across the whole

business system. Decisions on structure and human resources should flow directly from strategic requirements.

A hopeless case?

So what do you do if your strategic analysis convinces you that your company is in a weak position in a declining industry? One answer is to sell it to someone who has a rosier view or better economics.

In many declining industries there is a healthy process of consolidation underway so your, relatively weak, company might be truly more valuable to someone else than to your current shareholders.

If, for example, you own three independent coffee shops in a mid-sized town which are showing losses in the face of competition from Starbucks, there is a pretty good chance those shops are worth more to Starbucks than to you. They buy their coffee, tea and food much cheaper than you can. Their staff training is spread across a large group of stores. They can afford national advertising. Chances are, they will make more profit from your shops than you can. But it will be time consuming for Starbucks simply to compete you out, so a mutually desirable deal should be possible and your best strategy is to sell and put the money into something new.

Moving from vision to strategy

A corporate vision may not describe a purely commercial objective but a business strategy needs to turn that objective into profitable operations. In Chapter 3, I gave details of how well-known businesses link strategy to vision. Here are two more examples.

BIG MAC MAKES BIG PROFITS FROM BRICKS AND MORTAR

The driving force behind McDonald's – Ray Kroc – had the *vision* of taking what had been a one-off hamburger restaurant in California into a national chain by means of franchising.

However for many of the early years he made little or no profit as, although the franchises paid him an upfront fee and a small annual percentage of sales, this was not enough to do much more than cover his central costs.

The breakthrough came in the late 1950s when McDonald's set up the Franchise Reality Corporation, which acquired sites and then leased them back to franchisees at a big mark-up. This provided more control over franchises and transformed the economics by giving McDonald's Corporation much better margins. The *strategy* was to use the new mechanism to charge the franchisees for the value created by the parent company.[2]

LEASE, NOT SALE, WAS THE SECRET FOR XEROX

A small company from Rochester, New York, pioneered the Xerox copying machine. It used a new process – which they called 'xerography' – to produce copies of documents on ordinary paper.

This *vision* was of all offices being equipped with plain-paper copying machines, but in the 1950s almost all office equipment was mechanical and low cost and the highly complex Xerox looked hugely expensive.

The *strategy* that made this work was to lease the machine and charge users a few cents for each copy they made. It was this approach that led to success. At an initial price of nearly $30,000 in 1960 the Xerox 914 (the first machine) was far too costly for most offices to purchase. However, a monthly rental of just under $100 was not a barrier and the few cents per copy seemed cheap given the alternative of re-typing by hand.[3]

In an office market where most machinery had been sold outright, it was a bold move, but it was the leasing and pay-as-you-go strategy as much as the original invention that created the ultimate success.

Staying flexible

A company's strategy cannot and should not be set in stone. Strategy is a broad description of goals, not a narrow prescription of activity. A company cannot undertake a strategic review every five years and feel that it has 'done strategy'. It is a dynamic, not a static process.

A good strategy sets the context within which the right tactical actions can be taken and it lets managers know the broad corporate direction. Jack Welch, General Electric's CEO, described strategy as 'a central idea – a simple core concept'. In an appendix to his autobiography, *Jack*, he quotes from a letter written by a planning manager to *Fortune* magazine talking about strategy in the context of the ideas of the Prussian General Karl von Clausewitz, who wrote the seminal strategic text *On War* in 1832:

> Von Clausewitz summed up what it had all been about in his classic 'On War'. Men could not reduce strategy to a formula. Detailed planning necessarily failed, due to the inevitable frictions encountered: chance events, imperfections in execution, and the independent will of the opposition. Instead, the human elements were paramount: leadership, morale, and the almost instinctive savvy of the best generals.
>
> The Prussian general staff, under the elder von Moltke, perfected these concepts in practice. They did not expect a plan of operations to survive beyond the first contact with the enemy. They set only the broadest of objectives and emphasised seizing unforeseen opportunities as they arose. *Strategy was not a lengthy action plan. It was the evolution of a central idea through continually changing circumstances.*
>
> Business and war may differ in objectives and codes of conduct. But both involve facing the independent will of other parties. Any cookbook approach is

powerless to cope with independent will, or with the
unfolding situations of the real world.[4]

The italics were added by Mr Welch to stress the approach that he
followed in GE. Using strategy as a guiding principle rather than a
fixed set of rules.

A chief executive who develops a highly detailed and ridged strategy is making the same error as one who is too involved in micro
management. It has the effect of de-motivating and undermining operating managers who, rather than trying to solve problems, simply
look for the answer in the 'strategy manual'.

Formulating a strategy is based on asking questions, but those
questions must continue to be asked and the strategic plan must be
subject to constant interrogation and, when required, change. The
corporate vision may be a constant and bedrock, but the strategy
should reflect shifting sands and changing currents.

Summary

- An enterprise has a strategy to grow and generate cash, not
  simply to exist.
- CEOs lead and control the development of a strategy but must
  involve other managers.
- Strategy formulation is all about asking questions and forming a
  view of what the future will look like for the economy, the
  industry and the company itself.
- Generic strategies do not work and each company has to come up
  with a coherent plan which reflects its own unique circumstances.
- A strategy is only of value if it is clearly communicated to all the
  people in a business and is implemented across the whole
  business system.
- The corporate strategy must be flexible and respond to changing
  conditions and opportunities.

5

Ensuring accountability: structure

The structure of a company should serve its strategy and reflect its geographic requirements. It should be flexible and modified when changes in strategy require it. A structure works well when it provides clear accountability so that everyone knows who is their boss and people feel a strong sense of ownership of their business unit. The main skill of the CEO is not in designing a perfect structure – there is no such thing – but in making a structure work.

Structure is about who does what to whom and is a mechanism for allocating resources into logical and manageable groups. It gives people a 'map' of where they are. It gives context and shows who to ask for what to get things done.

The structure of a company is much less solid and set in stone than the word might suggest. It should be fluid and flexible and follow on from strategy rather than be allowed to dictate it.

Structure is, unfortunately, a political issue and therefore resolving conflict about it has to be a top down decision where the CEO takes account of the various trade-offs. In any structural change some win and some lose. Some gain power, some have it taken away. However, determining the most effective structure from a design point of view is a bottom-up process based on understanding what the business is trying to achieve.

Discussions of structure bring out the worst in people and can create substantial tensions. On several occasions in my own career I have been forced to become involved in assigning offices to senior people. Normally rational individuals become obsessed with things like views, size of windows and quality of soft furnishings. It is a maddening situation, but in the end only the 'boss' can resolve such issues. The decisions about organisational titles are even more sensitive and political than those about office location.

Small businesses are easy to structure. There is the managing director who makes decisions, the finance director who counts the money, the sales director who finds customers and the people who do the work. Big businesses are made up of small businesses. The issue is how to fit those small businesses together in a way that works. Structure is to business what plumbing is to a house. It is necessary, but you do not really want it on display all the time.

Structure is important to individuals because it defines their role and, through that, their status and power. Ask yourself how interested you are in the organisation chart of your own company? Of course you are – you want to know where you sit in the overall hierarchy and who does what to whom. You want to know where the power lies and how resources are allocated. The structure chart gives a good idea of how the politics function.

But what do you care for the organisational chart of a supplier? Does it matter to you how the staff of your hotel or airline are organised? You want responsive service from the check-in desk at the airport or the airline stewardess. You do not ask if the person processing your telephone booking is a clerk, a supervisor or the managing director. You will judge them on results, not their title or to whom they report.

The organisation chart of a customer company may be more important to you as it can tell who are the decision makers and, therefore, the most attractive prospects for your sales pitch. But beyond that, again, you do not care that much. Structure is an internal issue.

The structure of a business should be designed to achieve its strategic goals and to make the best use of resources. Unfortunately structure is often a function of some long-forgotten historical accident and frequently is a politically driven solution, shaped by the demands and power, perceived and real, of senior executives.

In the real world reporting relationships are arranged to reflect personalities. Also whole divisions are created to provide a job for 'good old Bob', who is the CEO's best friend and just too expensive to fire. Head-office staff functions are created as a retirement home for politically powerful yet ineffective line managers. Ambitious vice presidents build large internal staff departments because they feel the number of employees who report to them is an important personal career benchmark.

CEOs must control and dictate structure and should be constantly asking questions about the way things are organised. Nearly all the other people in the company will want a structure which suits them personally. It is the CEO who must decide what is right for the business overall.

Elements of structure

There is a rich literature on the theory of organisational design. Early ideas originated from military thinking and were then modified by the demands of the industrial revolution. Modern management really started less than a century ago with Henry Ford's notion of the assembly line to create ultra-specialised tasks. This was being introduced about the same time as F. W. Taylor published his groundbreaking ideas in *The Principles of Scientific Management*.[1]

Changes in society and improvements in education mean much of the early thinking now looks like the organisational equivalent of building tower blocks for public housing. Good in theory but poor in practice. The reality is that human beings like to do jobs that give them some control over their lives and which have meaning to them. What may look perfect on a structure chart often results in a depressing or de-humanising job. Assigning specialists to tasks is still required, but not to the degree that the jobs created become wholly unrewarding and mechanical.

Almost every company, no matter how small, will follow some form of departmentalisation along the lines of

- sales,
- operations/production,
- finance/administration.

In a one-man firm obviously one person does all the tasks, but even then they will more or less consciously 'change hats' between roles. Most companies, of course, are much larger and, broadly, there are three ways to structure a complex commercial organisation. By

- product/service,
- function,
- geography.

In a product-led approach all functions and geographies (countries, states or towns) report into a product head. If a company has multiple products, it may well have separate business units in the same location. This should result in better products with the 'customer as king' but may lead to duplication of costs.

In the function-led approach all manufacturing, for example, may come under a common head irrespective of its location. This will be efficient in production terms but may lead to a lack of customer focus as the internal objectives become more important than market driven goals.

In the geography-led approach all of a company's activities will be grouped under a country or location manager. This may lead to lack of product focus but will result in operating efficiencies and shared resources.

Most large, international companies are a mixture of all three and are commonly called 'matrix organisations', meaning the leader of a particular business unit or department often reports to different people on different issues. The concept of 'brand manager' was invented to help manage across a matrix so that a shampoo, for example, had its worldwide product champion. The brand manager would try to get the best for his or her product from the production people, the marketing group and the local country managers.

In designing an organisation a CEO has to take account of a range of issues as described below.

Staff and line roles

The origins of the idea of line and staff jobs probably come from the military structure, where *line* meant the people in the fighting units and *staff* were the HQ administration group. It is increasingly taken to mean the distinction between line people who work in customer- or supplier-facing roles (sales, operations) and those in the administrative, central staff jobs. It can also imply the difference between people who work in business units (line) and those in the corporate centre working on strategy and development (staff).

For me, it is most useful to distinguish those managers who are responsible for managing other people as line and those who, whilst doing very senior jobs, really only have to worry about themselves or a very small team as staff.

As organisations become more 'virtual' and more functions are outsourced there is an increasing percentage of senior people who manage large amounts of corporate resources but are not in conventional line roles. A manager, for example, who controls marketing and advertising may have a budget of tens of millions of dollars but might be thought of as staff rather than line as she only has one assistant reporting to her.

As a broad generalisation, smart people can do either line or staff jobs. But good line managers need an extra set of skills with personnel to help them deal with the needs, demands and concerns of their direct employees.

Pivotal jobs

Some job functions play a vital role in making a company successful. Abolish the job or have it done badly and wheels start to drop off the corporate wagon. The existence of a *pivotal job* is a function of an organisation's structure. It is not a comment on the indispensability or otherwise of an individual in the role. It is the job itself that is key to making the company function well because of its interface with other functions.

Typically general managers or managing directors of business units have pivotal jobs, not simply because they control a stream of profits or costs but because they manage the interaction between the business units and other parts of the company. They manage trade-offs and potential conflicts. Similarly, sales directors may be in a pivotal role if they set prices and have to negotiate with operations managers to produce the right goods at the right time.

Most aspects of production, operations, sales and finance are important, but not pivotal in this sense because the way the job is done does not make a crucial difference to the company's overall performance. Good operations people can save costs and good sales people will improve revenues, but they can do this almost in isolation. Their functions are valuable, but not *pivotal*.

If you have a poor performer in many managerial jobs you will have a less than perfect performance. A poor performer in a pivotal job will lead to major difficulties. Figure 5.1 shows the way that the managing director of a country division has a pivotal job. There will be potential conflicts of interest between global and local suppliers (which is in the best interests of overall business versus which is best for the business unit) and also face similar issues with customers.

People in these jobs must possess a wide range of skills, including interpersonal and negotiating abilities, rather than mere functional expertise. These appointments must be made with great care.

Figure 5.1   **Pivotal jobs**

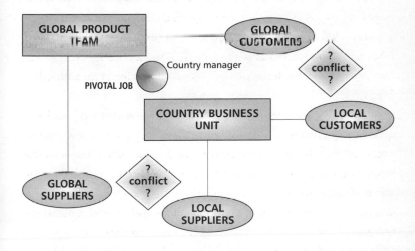

Span of control

This, essentially, is a question of how many direct reports an individual can handle.

The vast majority of people have a boss, someone who has the power to hire and fire them, who sets salary and bonuses and makes personnel decisions. In addition, that boss is involved in approving decisions made by direct reports. A good and effective boss or line manager must be available to his or her team not just to be consulted on business issues but also to discuss with them their own career plans, personnel and, where appropriate, personal problems. If someone has too many direct reports they will be spread too thinly and their value as a counsellor and confidant will rapidly diminish.

My own instinct is that ten direct reports is about all anyone can really handle. If someone reports to you then you must find time for him or her. To help them solve problems, to provide feedback, listen to their tales of woe and share their triumphs. Also to be available to lead the search for a replacement if they leave.

If anyone has more than ten direct reports, something is probably wrong with the structure.

Loose/tight organisation

A constant dilemma for a CEO is how to encourage innovation and entrepreneurial risk taking by business-unit managers whilst keeping tight control and providing central direction. A culture which requires head office approval for almost any decision will stifle initiative. On the other hand, too much freedom and a lack of systems to monitor financial performance can lead to accounting black holes and nasty surprises.

The most widely adopted solution is strict financial controls, which may even extend to daily cash balances and detailed weekly sales and cost reports, combined with a high degree of autonomy for managers and employees and which allows local decision making.

This is really more an issue of organisational systems and culture than structure but *tight* financial controls do not stifle initiative and provide accountability within a *loose* management culture. This is covered in more detail under 'Tactics' in Chapter 7.

Balance and tension

A suspension bridge works because of the balancing of the tensions inherent in the structure. The same is true for an organisation.

Even in a simple, small business the sales team are likely to be at odds with the production people. Sales will want product modifications and a wide product range to suit every possible customer. Production will want to standardise everything to keep costs down.

In a multi-business unit, multinational company there is always the issue of whether to organise by geography or by line of business. The corporate centre will usually fight with the operations. Business units will want their own R&D to ensure local solutions. The corporate team will want to centralise R&D to achieve economies. The group finance director will want central purchasing to capture volume discounts. The divisional MDs will want local purchasing to get better customer service.

It is a constant task for the CEO and the holders of pivotal jobs to manage these types of trade-off. However, trying to design an organisation in such a way that all the tensions are removed can be counterproductive, as it results in too great a focus on production or sales when it is the very existence of the balance that makes the business work well. Achieving the correct balance and managing the tension is greatly helped by the CEO being very clear about who runs what and who reports to whom.

Clarity of role

People need to know who their boss is, to whom they report and who sets their salary and bonus. They want to know what their job is.

When designing a structure, account must be taken of all the processes that a business needs to carry out and the charts should provide clear guidance as to who does what in each process. Structure should ensure that people are accountable for their actions and feel a sense of responsibility. Everyone who works in an organisation should be able to clearly say, 'I work for Business Unit X which is run by Manager Y'.

This approach also ensures that people have nowhere to hide. Each person is part of a unit which can be monitored and observed and which can be seen to be making profits or losses. However, there can be times when some ambiguity is desirable, particularly if two strong individuals both make a significant contribution to success but neither is prepared to consider the other their boss. If making a structure too clear creates tensions it is sometimes better to leave things a little opaque as long as the business functions well.

This is one more example of why structure is not as solid as it sounds.

The business unit

At the heart of organisational structure for larger concerns is the idea of business units. The business unit is the key building block of a large company. It allows a large business to keep focused on various markets whilst enjoying the benefits of scale.

A business unit is usually, or could be, a business in its own right. It has an identifiable market, its own customers, its own employees and suppliers. It is a business that its boss can 'get their arms round'. It should have its own recognisable income and costs and should be able to produce its own profit-and-loss account and balance sheet if required. It should be able to stand alone as a business in its own right if its parent company were to sell it.

In large companies business units may receive support and service from other business units or from the corporate centre. Things like IT, research and development, finance or public relations. But this is no different from them buying in these services from third-party suppliers.

It is possible to have a business unit of just one person. In a law firm you could argue that each partner is a business unit in his or her own right. In reality, it never works this way, but business units can be quite small and still be viable.

An identified individual must lead a business unit and that person should be encouraged to think like a chief executive and an entrepreneur. They need to feel they 'own' the business unit and will be rewarded for its success and held accountable for its failure.

When to have a business unit

A business unit should be created when it addresses a market the company wishes to serve. Having too few business units may result in them being too big and too broad, ill defined and unwieldy. Their managers and staff will feel lost. But having too many will create duplications of cost and can produce too many 'business barons', which creates additional complexities of reporting and control.

A business unit will have its own sub-departments which group together particular skills in terms of recruitment, training and line management. These departments typically include:

- sales,
- operations,
- manufacturing/supply,
- administration.

The business unit is not a new idea. In his analysis of Standard Oil (the forerunner of Exxon and Esso) in the 1880s Daniel Gross commented:

> The smooth functioning of the whole was predicated on the reliable performance of every constituent unit. Thus, while granting the subsidiaries a degree of autonomy the central administration imposed substantial requirements on them. Each Standard unit was expected to show a profit on its own for example … and had imposed on them uniform financial reporting requirements.[2]

Business units as a mechanism for focus

All business units do not need to be trading entities seeking to make profits. If an organisation needs to be very good at something, it may make sense for that 'something' to be addressed by a business unit.

McDonald's, for example, needed to train its store managers and does so by the use of its 'Hamburger University'. The training team are regarded as a business unit or cost centre. Likewise, GE under Jack Welch placed great store on its training centre at Crotonville to help create a culture and build skills. Again, I am sure it was run by a senior leader and could be thought of as a business unit. Similarly, a company which relies on flat-screen technology, for example, may well set up a business unit to manufacture or purchase it.

Business units can be a very efficient way to run a group of people whether they are profit centres or not.

Business units as cost centres

Some functions need to be organised as a business unit but they do not make a product or service that can be sold to an outside customer. Things like public relations, internal legal services, R&D, information technology and international tax may need to be grouped into business units to provide focus and scale.

The skill is to ensure that these 'non-profit' units are run in a client-focused and lean way by managers who have the right personal characteristics. These are not typical entrepreneurial business-unit leaders but need a well-developed sense of customer service and politics. They must operate with more complex success criteria than simply 'grow your profits'.

An internal market between business units

When business units buy services from third-party suppliers they can be reasonably sure they get good prices – by going out to tender – and that they get good service by firing suppliers who underperform. Problems arise when it is decided at a corporate level that wholly owned business units will act as suppliers to each other without the ability to 'test the market'.

The most simplistic approach is to say that internal would-be suppliers are asked to bid in the open market against third-party companies for contracts. It is great in theory but overlooks the fact that for the corporation as a whole the best economic solution may well be to leave the contract with the internal group even if the 'customer' business unit ends up paying more.

Typical examples might be a multi-location newspaper publisher that has its own printing capacity, or a multi-branch bank that has its own internal marketing unit.

But the issue can also extend to, for example, IT departments and even accounting teams. Business unit general managers will often be frustrated with services received from other parts of their own corporation, as they will feel they are being forced to accept second best rather than seeking the ideal solution in the open market outside.

Corporate parents need a structural solution to ensure that at some point in the line management structure both the 'customer' and the 'supplier' business units come under the control of a single line manager who can intervene if the relationship is not working. Also the managers of the suppliers need to have some of their remuneration linked to satisfaction levels shown by their internal customers.

In large companies the business units will need to 'trade' with each other as well as fulfilling their main role of selling products and services externally. A typical solution is to structure things as an internal market where central service units charge other businesses units for work done. Having such costs appear on their P&L makes the business unit general managers very demanding customers and forces the service units to have a customer mentality.

Coordinating business units

The stronger the focus of the individual business units on their own issues, and the more autonomous the managers, then the more difficult it becomes to get them to cooperate on various issues.

The role of chief operating officer is frequently created to attempt to force business unit cooperation. If cooperation is not forthcoming, there is a danger of a raft of coordinator jobs being created in the corporate centre (marketing, sales, purchasing, development, etc.) to try to get the various businesses working together. This is usually ineffective and expensive. The best solution is to make some element of the business unit manager's remuneration linked to cooperation.

Country managers

One of the questions most often posed about structure is whether countries should be business units in their own right. The most complex organisational challenge for many companies is expansion beyond their home market. Many industries have 'gone global' and growth strategies dictate that companies are present in many markets.

Consumer goods companies that have invested hundreds of millions of dollars into products and brands need to recapture the fixed cost through worldwide sales. Advertising agencies that work for these consumer goods clients must have global networks of offices to provide service in each market. Accounting firms need a worldwide network to service their clients. The question then becomes one of how to organise those various markets. The conventional answer is the 'country manager'.

In many multinational companies each country becomes automatically recognised as a business unit. The country manager enjoys a great deal of power and autonomy. In many cases, it seems, too much. More than any other structure this runs the risk of creating empires and of establishing leaders and teams who are so possessive about their own territory that they resent fitting in with the overall corporation. *The Economist* quoted a senior executive in a multinational as saying, 'It was like medieval England: the barons were much more powerful than the king. As a result, we had a lot of little companies aligned under a single name.'[3]

The Economist also reported that in the 1990s many companies had tried to reduce the power of country managers and centralise more of the decision-making but that, subsequently, companies were thinking of putting power back to the local manager for fear of losing touch with the national markets.[4]

IBM's Lou Gerstner was shocked at what he found when he took over in 1993:

> IBMers practically had to ask permission to enter the
> territory of a Country Manager. Each country had its
> own independent system. Employees belonged to their
> geographic first while IBM took a distant second place.
> I declared war on the geographic fiefdoms. I decided
> we would organise the company around global industry
> teams.[5]

Companies that are wholly centralised will find it much harder to
stay in touch with and respond to local markets and will find it hard
to recruit and retain talent. Good people normally want to enjoy a
sense of autonomy and do not like to feel their real boss is 3,000
miles away. However, a company which leaves everything in the
hands of its country managers may fail to capture economies of scale
and end up duplicating many costs as it keeps re-inventing the wheel.
The reality is that the correct answer must be some form of balance.
It is not so much the structure but the way people choose to operate
it.

The fact is that most countries really ARE different from their
neighbours. Laws, currencies, cultures, business practices, education, attitudes are all different. Frustrating though it may be for the
tidy minded in the corporate centre, a business must reflect these
local conditions. Being in more than one market inevitably produces
tensions and conflicts.

- The local general manager wants to maximise sales and profits of
  her business unit. The global product manager wants to
  maximise sale of his product using the countries as a conduit.
- The local general manager wants to buy supplies from the
  cheapest/best source with the best local service. The global
  procurement manager wants to put in place global deals to
  capture extra discounts.
- The local general manager wants to establish price points that

he feels will maximise sales in his market. The central
marketing director wants a global pricing policy to maximise
overall sales.

The United Nations problem

In the UN all countries have an equal vote irrespective of size or economic power. But countries really are accidents of history, geography, culture and war. There is no logic to it. In multinational
companies similar anomalies can arise.

France, with a population of nearly 60 million, a land mass of
540,000 square kilometres and a GDP of some $1,500 billion, is a
country. So is Ireland, which has 3.5 million people, occupies
70,000 square kilometres and has a GDP of about $100 billion. Po-
litically there is no doubt that each is a self-governing state, but if
they were business units in a company, would you accord each one
the same organisational status?

Many companies structure business units around countries as logical geographic boundaries but it creates some odd effects. National
economies vary greatly in size and a business with a big market share
in a small country may be much smaller and less economically
important than one with a small share of a big country.

In a business the main determinants of importance are, or should
be, the size of the operation in terms of sales and growth potential –
not its national status. But, in fact, go to most multinationals' management conferences and you will see many more people from small
markets than big ones, reflecting the UN problem.

The right design

There is no 'right' answer to structure. The solution will change over
time as a company grows and evolves, as customers and competitors
change, as technology brings new opportunities and threats. No one
design is inherently better or more effective than another. The skill

lies not so much in picking a structure but in making the one you
have picked work well.

The objectives of a structural solution are to:

- address the markets the strategy defines as important,
- make managers clear about responsibilities – who controls what,
- have a manageable span of control, i.e. not too many business
  units reporting to one person,
- assist business units to work with each other when required.

The vision and strategy must be clear, as the structure must serve the
strategy. If the strategy calls for success in a particular market, the
structure must address that market with the creation of a business
unit.

If a food manufacturer decides to target hypermarkets as clients,
it probably needs a business unit focused on this sector. If it decides
to focus on online shopping, again, a focused business unit will make
success more likely. If an airline decides that the business traveller is
key, it might set up a business unit to serve them. Or set one up to
focus on the crucial London–New York route.

As a general in a hypothetical army, you might command 500 infantry, fifty machine gunners and five artillery crews. How you de-
ploy them will depend on what the enemy is up to, the lie of the land,
even the weather. The total resource remains the same. The overall
objective is to win. How the troops are used will vary. The general
who always uses the same formation will not record many victories.
Structure must be flexible.

A critical point is that once an organisation has more than one
business unit, the task of the CEO is to manage *through* other people,
not the management *of* other people. This means creating business
units of which other managers have a sense of ownership.

TWO WAYS TO MAKE CARS

What is 'right' will change over time. Different structures produce different results in the market place, as is demonstrated by the car industry.

In the early days of automobile production, Ford had a wholly functional approach with an assembly line focused on churning out just Model Ts, which produced huge cost savings. General Motors, by contrast, was organised into product groups, which produced a much wider diversity of models.

To start with, GM suffered from high costs at a time when the public thirsted for cheap, mass-produced cars. GM lost out. But as public taste shifted to demand a wider range of alternatives, Ford began to suffer and lose market share, and the GM structure proved more effective.

Both structures worked for a time, each being more effective in different demand conditions.

A CHAIN OF SHOPS

Take the case of a number of convenience stores. Each shop is a business unit in its own right. It has its own customers and its own costs. It has a manager. It has its own set of accounts. There are no corporate politics. This type of shop can survive alone but increasingly they are grouped together in chains as the economics are better.

Assume now that ten shops, under common ownership, are located around a large city under a regional manager. This business may well choose to have a central accounting function and a central warehouse. The regional manager will have to control the internal services but it is unlikely that any individual shop manager would find this structure too difficult to operate. As stand-alone businesses they probably have relied on an external wholesaler. They probably also hired an external bookkeeper on a part-time basis so, in many ways, they probably now get better service from central functions which are 'in-house'.

But now assume that a major industry retailer buys up ten of these multi-shop chains. Now they have 100 shops all over the country and more difficult decisions to make:

- Do they have one central, national, warehouse which may reduce costs but could lead to long delivery delays and be less responsive?
- Do they have a single, national accounting office or does that make them lose face-to-face contact and familiarity with the stores?
- Do they keep a regional structure or do all shops report into a central manager?

Take it one step further and assume the corporate parent also owns a chain of supermarkets and a network of hotels.

Can you still have one accounting back office? Do you have regional managers who control all the business units in their region (convenience stores plus supermarkets plus hotels) or have three national managers (one for each chain) with apparently duplicated regional offices?

Should you demand that the confectionary and newspapers in the convenience stores come through the same system as that used for the food stores? Do you demand that all hotels buy their newspapers only from the sister chain of newsagents?

There are no easy answers. The best way forward is to pick the structure that feels right and then put in place mechanisms to overcome its weaknesses.

Summary

- There is no such thing as a 'right' structure. Designing the architecture of an organisation follows on from the strategy and reflects its geographic needs.
- A good structure should explain to people 'who does what to whom' and give people a sense of ownership of their own

business units. It should make it clear to people what their own
responsibilities are.

- An 'enterprise' needs its people to be entrepreneurial. The
  structure must encourage this by defining and delegating real
  responsibility and authority.
- The business unit is the key idea in organising large companies.
  Various mechanisms need to be put in place to help business
  units work successfully together.
- The CEO's role as 'chief architect' is to identify and manage all
  the numerous trade-offs that must be made in a structure and to
  put in place mechanisms to address the tensions and weaknesses
  that the structure throws up.

6

Finding talent: people

*Businesses cannot implement their strategy or operate their
structure without skilled and willing people. Recruiting people
is not just a matter of hiring them. Recruiting should take its
full meaning of recruiting them intellectually, emotionally and
legally. This means helping them identify with 'the cause' of
the company. It is also about retaining their interest and
motivating them once they have joined and increasing their
skills through training and coaching. CEOs have responsibility
for designing and implementing reward systems and setting the
style for people management.*

Finding talent in a business means getting the best employees and
getting the best out of them. It means helping them make the
most of their own abilities – finding their own hidden talents.

Management theorists go to great lengths to stress the importance
of people to a business and to offer advice on good practices in recruitment and retention. But the more I read, the more I suspect
some experts have had little experience of the real reasons why people come to work on a Monday morning. Many of the theories seem
to have a strong, politically correct agenda and fail to recognise the
reality of human behaviour.

With very few exceptions, people work because they want the
money. They need the money to live and to buy things. People want
to get paid as much as they can, which means most of our adult lives
are spent seeking a job that allows us to sell our talents to the
employment market for the maximum amount.

Now this does not mean that cash is the only motivation: far from
it. Working conditions, career prospects, corporate culture, personal

satisfaction, perceived glamour of the industry and the sense of doing something worthwhile – all these play a part in keeping people happy and motivated, but it would be wrong to lose sight of the importance of money. Job satisfaction comes from many things, but money is a tangible reward and the yardstick by which we all keep score.

People have the legitimate right to expect their managers (and by implication their CEO) to create a working environment in which they are respected and valued and which allows them to maximise their own earning potential.

The value of talent

For good or ill the human race distributes itself into a bell curve in almost all attributes: height, weight, IQ, motivation. At either end of the curve a small percentage of people are in an extreme group. The very tall and the very short, the very heavy and the very light are at the edges. But most of us are somewhere in the middle.

The challenge for a business is to make sure it has more than its fair share of employees on the positive side of the chart when it comes to ability and effort. These people will simply be more effective. They will sell harder, they will operate more efficiently, they will be sick less often.

A business can buy in better people by selective recruitment and high pay, but it can also produce its own by means of good training and motivation. As human beings, our position in the bell curve of 'effective employees' will vary over time and will be influenced by coaching and teaching. It's not just about who we are but how we are treated. People who are treated well do better.

Coaching

Clear instructions are the mark of a good manager. Coaching is the mark of a great manager.

A good coach can identify weaknesses in someone's skill-set and

help that person to overcome them. Coaching requires very open relationships and a high degree of trust. When the relationship is really
good, the coaching works both ways. I have learned a lot about new
software from people who work for me. Often the younger and
more recently graduated they are, the more they have to teach. My
ability to find things on the internet has come largely from 'upward'
coaching. Also, my knowledge of the right way to do business in what
are, to me, foreign cultures like China, Singapore and South Africa
has come through coaching from local managers.

I particularly remember being helped to make a speech in French
to several hundred very French staff in a provincial town. The French
company president (who reported to me) taught me all the right id-
ioms and ideas and he even tape-recorded the speech himself to give
me guidance of the nuances of accent. He made the event a success
and taught me a great deal.

It is of particular importance that the CEO is a good coach as this
will usually encourage the same behaviour in the senior team and will
lead to a coaching culture throughout the business. This, in turn,
makes a company more able to learn as an organisation.

The trickle-down effect

One role of the CEO is to set the style by which the business manages its people. The *way* that the CEO manages his or her direct reports will have a significant impact on the *way* those people manage
their direct reports and therefore on the whole management culture
of the business. If the CEO has a macho, take-no-prisoners approach, this will become the business norm. If the CEO has a strong
coaching style, then that will become prevalent.

People do not work for organisations. They work for other people.
An individual's enjoyment of, and effectiveness in, a job is linked much
more closely to the person they report to than it is to the company for
which they work. Although companies have their own rules, standards,
procedures, customs and culture, it is the direct relationships and the

way they are treated that most affect an individual's performance.

The way CEOs treat their direct reports will have a disproportionate impact on the way the rest of the people in the organisation are treated. Rules have far less impact than observed behaviour. As Christian Hath, the CEO of the large American grocery store chain A&P, said, 'People don't work for the company but for the direct boss they are engaged with. I can't be in every store everyday but I can create the right kind of manager.'[1]

CEOs must recognise their own value as role models and consciously create an attitude and approach that they wish to see adopted by all their managers.

Making people happy

We all know that people work more effectively when they are happy, but how can managers achieve this? The first step is to create an attractive corporate image. Some companies seem far more desirable as employers than others.

Corporate image

What makes a company an attractive employer is a mix of many aspects. A typical list of attributes is that used by the survey *The 100 Best Companies to Work for in Canada*:[2]

- Pay
- Benefits
- Promotion prospects
- Job security
- Atmosphere
- Job satisfaction
- Communications
- Personal development

There are many other lists published and those based on employee surveys frequently find that non-financial issues are the most important: flexible working hours and products that people are proud of, for example.

Companies that have great reputations are magnets for talented people. It is yet one more reason to spend time and money on making your business famous. In his book *Living the Brand* Nicholas Ind comments:

> While having a strong external reputation is important
> for recruitment, it is also an important element in the
> retention of people. The way people think an
> organisation is seen by others is important for their
> self-esteem. It's always better if people say 'Wow!'
> when you explain who you work for, than if they look
> sympathetic and say 'Who?'[3]

I believe this idea of linking a company's attractiveness as an employer to such a response at a cocktail party or in a bar is very important.

I worked for many years for the BBC, which paid me very little for my labours. However, I do not think I have ever been happier in a job in terms of feeling I was using my time well. A big part of that was the reaction of strangers when social conversation turned, as it always does, to 'for whom do you work?' When I said, 'The BBC,' the response was usually, 'Tell me more.' It felt good to be part of a well-regarded organisation.

Every year the San Francisco based Great Places to Work Institute conducts a detailed survey of the world's best companies to work for. Although pay is a major factor, they report that many cultural aspects of a business, such as the products it makes and the level of equality, have a big impact.

One of the co-founders of the Institute, Robert Levering, wrote:

At Nestlé, for example, many people could make more
money elsewhere. But employees like being with a
company whose mission is to feed the world. At
Bacardi Martini in Britain they appreciate working for a
company with a commitment to quality. Egalitarianism
is another theme. Intel in Ireland has brought the
Silicon Valley culture of no reserved parking spaces and
no executive dining rooms.[4]

The Great Place to Work web site[5] contains a phrase they feel
encapsulates the essence of a great workplace:

You TRUST the people you work for, have PRIDE in
what you do and ENJOY the people you work with.

Employee engagement

The Gallup Organisation is famous for its opinion polls but has also
tuned its skills to understanding employee motivation. It interviewed
more than a million employees to understand more about the relationship between people and their organisations.

Gallup found that the majority of people were what it called
'ROAD warriors' – Retired On Active Duty – who simply carried
out their tasks but were not really 'engaged' in their work. The best
companies had the fewest of this type of person.

Gallup has formulated twelve questions – which they call Q12[6] –
that they say will reveal if employees are really engaged by their work
(Figure 6.1). People are asked to rank their response from 'strongly
agree' to 'strongly disagree'. The greater the agreement, the stronger
the workplace. A strong workplace led to lower staff turnover, better
customer satisfaction and improved organisational performance. If
employees are not 'engaged', managers must find out why and take
steps to improve the relationship.

Figure 6.1   **Gallup's Q12: engaged employees**
(copyright © The Gallup Organisation 2001)

1 Do I know what is expected of me at work?
2 Do I have the materials and equipment I need to do my work right?
3 At work, do I have the opportunity to do what I do best every day?
4 In the last seven days, have I received recognition or praise for doing good work?
5 Does my supervisor, or someone at work, seem to care about me as a person?
6 Is there is someone at work who encourages my development?
7 At work, do my opinions seem to count?
8 Does the mission/purpose of my company make me feel like my work is important?
9 Are my co-workers committed to doing quality work?
10 Do I have a best friend at work?
11 In the last six months, have I talked with someone at work about my progress?
12 This last year, have I had opportunities at work to learn and grow?

Unequal treatment

All men and women may well be created equal in terms of human rights but they certainly do not deserve equal treatment in terms of rewards in the workplace.

Some people simply add more value in their jobs either because they have more talent or because they work harder or because they are lucky or, often, all three. The big performers must receive the big rewards. Overall it will make employees *un*happy if they see that their business carries passengers and that underperformers get positive rewards. People need to see success being recognised and failings addressed.

In their best-selling book *Execution: The Discipline of Getting Things Done* Larry Bossidy and Ram Charan go to great lengths to stress that reward structures must differentiate the good performer from both the average and the bad. They also highlight the fact that many business leaders are very reluctant to give staff bad news:

Too many behave like wimps. We've seen again and

again that people love to give rewards; they love to be
loved. But they don't have the emotional fortitude to
give honest feedback and either withhold a reward or
penalize people. They don't feel comfortable rewarding
performance and behaviour. Leaders sometimes even
create new jobs for non-performers.[7]

People who are underperformers must be told so and, if possible,
must be told why. That way they may be able to improve, if it is in
their control, or look for a different job relationship which will create a better fit and allow them to maximise their performance. If
they continue to fail they must be removed, as failure has a major
negative impact on the morale of the rest of the company.

General Electric adopts what some people consider the rather
brutal approach of identifying each year the top 20 per cent of executives, who get promotions, options and bonuses, the middle 70 per
cent, who are regarded as the vital heart of the business and told so,
and the bottom 10 per cent of 'underperformers', who are likely to
get fired. The CEO Jack Welch commented:

Performance management has been part of everyone's
life from the first grade. Differentiation applies to
football teams, cheerleading squads, and honor societies.
It applies to the college admissions process. It applies at
graduation. There's differentiation for all of us in our
first 20 years. Why should it stop in the workplace?[8]

Reward should reflect contribution, not seniority or job title. The assessment of contribution needs to be as scientific and objective as possible. People who are doing outstandingly must be rewarded outstandingly.

Psychological contract
Most managers have a contract of employment which lays out the

legal framework for the relationship between themselves and their company. This contract governs the relationship in strict legal terms, but there is an equally important emotional relationship, sometimes called the psychological contract, which determines whether employees are happy at work and if they feel they are being fairly treated.

People who feel they have been passed over for promotion or who feel they are not given proper respect, or even who feel their office is too small, will almost certainly have no legal grounds for complaint but may become highly disaffected and be in breach of their emotional contract.

A good line manager will find ways to review this employee–company relationship and take steps to try to ensure that the psychological contract is honoured, if only by talking through the perceived grievance with the person concerned to see if there is any real basis in fact.

Recruitment

Most businesses are continually hiring new staff. The company may be growing and need more resources. Existing people retire, are lured elsewhere, move away or sometimes have to be fired.

Bringing in a new recruit is an opportunity to upgrade the skills in a business and to introduce new talent. The risk is that a great deal of money is spent on advertising, headhunting fees and induction costs, only to discover that the new individual is a failure.

To be successful at recruitment, a company must answer three questions:

- What does the post actually require?
- What type of person do we want?
- What are the key signs that show a person will fit in?

More than anything, successful recruitment is about fit. Matching job characteristics to personal characteristics; tasks with skills, and prospects with ambitions.

A recruitment mistake reflects far more badly on the company than it does on the individual. It is the company that designed and managed the recruitment process, and the company that must take most of the blame if it goes wrong.

Clarity of proposition

When advertising for staff, briefing search consultants, designing a vacancies web page or interviewing candidates, managers need to be as clear as possible about what the company does and what the proposed job involves within that context.

Recruitment is a two-way process and the more honest the company and its managers are about what is really needed, the more likely it is that the selected candidate will be a success. If managers give job seekers a clear idea of what's on offer, the candidates are that much more likely to be able to recognise themselves in the role. The best appointments are almost self-selecting.

Many jobs have ill-defined parameters in terms of responsibilities and turf rules. People sense this even in an interview and will shy away from uncertainty and confusion. They want to know it's a real job with real responsibilities. If you have designed a bad position do not be surprised if you cannot find good people to do it.

So, well before looking for candidates, make absolutely sure that the job being offered makes sense.

Square pegs

People are all different. Jobs are different. Obvious statements, but often apparently ignored in the recruitment processes of many companies.

It is very difficult to change the underlying character, skills, attitudes and behaviour of individuals. In truth, it is far easier to move people into redesigned jobs that suit them rather than to change the person to suit the job.

Chatty extroverts do make good salespeople. Focused introverts do make good financial controllers. It may be obvious, but companies are forever trying to fit square pegs into round holes because they do not ask enough questions about the individuals or about the nature of the job they are being asked to do.

DELIVERING SUPERIOR SERVICE

In a service business like the hotel industry, the behaviour of employees is a crucial factor for success. The Four Seasons, which tops many hotel-service surveys, places huge emphasis on recruitment. Isadore Sharpe, the founder of Four Seasons, says: 'It's easy to train someone to do a job, but it's very hard to train someone with a poor attitude to be highly motivated.'[9]

To ensure they have the right attitude, every employee – from dishwasher to senior manager – has four or five interviews before being hired. The editor of the *Hideaway Guide* to top hotels comments: Four Seasons seems to have a better instinct for picking the correct employees. It may have nothing to do with your credentials or experience; just something they can spot about you based on enthusiasm or sincerity.[10]

The reward package

Most employees should have three elements to their financial reward package.

- Salary
- Short-term bonus
- Long-term incentive

The skill is to balance these three between short- and long-term performance goals.

Salary

Salary is driven by market forces. What is the minimum amount I can pay to get you to come to work for me? So 'how much' is really a question of how much are other people prepared to pay for the same person. In many ways, then, salary does not reflect performance. It is driven more by a person's age, experience and the market value of their skill set.

A profit-sharing plan is not really a personal performance bonus, as most recipients have little or no personal impact on profits, so it is simply a variable adjunct to salary. It is a sharing in success rather than a direct reward for individual performance.

Profit-sharing plans make part of the salary profit linked and thus reduce the fixed-cost base. They are increasingly used in professional service firms where salary is by far the largest cost.

Short-term bonus

Gilbert and Sullivan's *Mikado* made famous the idea of 'making the punishment fit the crime'. Making the reward fit the job done well is easy in theory, difficult in practice.

A bonus is a payment for achieving some short-term goal. It is normally a cash payment to mark hitting annual targets. It has to be enough to get the employee's attention and change behaviour. Anything less than about 10 per cent of annual salary is probably not much of a motivation.

Whatever the targets are, they have to be clear and must be set at the beginning of the year. Where people are selling something, it is straightforward. The idea of the sales commission has been around since business began: sell more and we pay you more. Other targets such as quality control or speed of processing are equally valid, but must be clearly defined and agreed by both manager and bonus recipient. The annual bonus must be closely linked into the annual assessment. People must know why they have done well or badly.

Long-term incentives

A long-term incentive serves a different role from an annual bonus. It is about rewarding people, usually senior people, for loyalty and for making the company more valuable. It is meant to align the interests of employees and shareholders.

Typically these rewards are paid out on longer-term achievements such as consistent profit growth or margin improvement over several years. They are often paid in shares which must be held for some years, and only have value if the long-term targets are met. This avoids the controversial stock options lottery.

Stock options

Stock options became almost a religion in Anglo-Saxon capitalism in the last two decades of the twentieth century. For example, in 1981 the value of vested options at GE was just $6 million. By 2000, some 32,000 employees had options with a potential value of $12 billion.[11] In 1992 1,300 IBM staff held options. By 2001 this had risen to 72,500.[12] Many senior managers became multi-millionaires through cashing in of shares.

The theory is that options align the interests of shareholders and managers by focusing both groups of people on growing the share price. The problem is that, in the long boom bull market on the world's stock exchanges, options started to have great value even if company performance was below average.

Managers realised huge windfall profits without effort. Worse, they realised too that some very short-term 'fixes' such as high-priced acquisitions and very aggressive accounting treatments boosted share prices even if they actually destroyed long-term value.

The academic regarded by some as the intellectual father of the stock options in the 1980s, Michael Jensen, was quoted in *The*

Economist in 2002 as saying that 'stock options have become managerial heroin'.[13]

Jensen suggested a new approach with customised options which are profitable to the manager only if the share price appreciates by more than the firm's cost of capital and which can be exercised only after a long time when it has become clear that the performance is sustainable.

In a stock market slump the opposite problem occurs and options have no value even if the manager and the company have outperformed, simply because share prices are all falling.

Tell them what they are *really* worth

Employees will often be tempted to work elsewhere. Most people have a sense that 'the grass is always greener over the hill'. The job market is no different from any other market. Prospective employers are 'selling' job offers and will do all they can to make them attractive.

Persuading people to join or stay with a company is not just a matter of rewarding them but ensuring they know what their ongoing employment is *really* worth to them.

Texas Instruments (TI) used a secure intranet site called to ensure that each employee had easy access to a file which showed them the exact, real-time value of their full employment package including salary, bonus, stock options, retirement plan and other perks. The magazine *Smart Business* reported:

> Show-me-the-money was the rallying cry of new-
> economy workers. Dot-com dementia had ramped up
> the demand for skilled workers and competitors
> offering hefty salaries and tempting stock-option
> packages were poaching some of TI's most valuable
> employees who when they quit took their skills – and
> TI's investment in their training – with them. They left

something behind them too: a lot of money. TI
executives were convinced employees left, in part,
because they just didn't know how much their
compensation packages were worth.[14]

TI's response was a clever use of their own secure intranet resources to enable employees to see the full current and potential future value of their jobs. It apparently made many people realise they
were better off where they were.

Information about the real value of the remuneration package and
how people are doing is the basis of a good working relationship.

Annual assessments

To be happy and successful in a job, people – no matter how senior
or smart – need feedback. They need to know how they are doing,
what is going right, what is going wrong and how they can improve
their performance. Companies also need to know how their people
are doing to identify skill shortages, assess training needs and plan
succession.

Annual assessment of staff is highly desirable. It is also highly time
consuming and, frequently, done very badly. The magazine *Management Today* reported:

> For a process that's so well established in the corporate
> landscape, the performance appraisal is astonishingly
> unpopular. Employees fear it as an annual calling-to-
> account, a sinister session where they'll have to defend
> their record, bat off criticism and make a desperate
> pitch for a pay rise. Managers, on the other hand, see it
> as a bureaucratic chore, an hour of ticking boxes and
> mouthing platitudes … According to the Institute of
> Personnel and Development one in eight managers

would actually prefer to visit the dentist than carry out a performance appraisal.[15]

CEOs must take the lead in operating a comprehensive assessment programme for their own direct reports in the hope and expectation that this approach will trickle down to the rest of the organisation. The comments that follow describe the way CEOs assess their direct reports, but they are valid for all managers.

Assessment criteria

There are unlimited ways of structuring and managing this process but most boil down to the same essentials. The typical annual process has three elements:

1   Developing objective assessment criteria.
2   Annual appraisal process including feedback from peers, subordinates and clients.
3   Annual face-to-face personal review.

For the assessment process to be open, transparent and equitable, people need to feel they are being judged by the same criteria as their peers. Typically, they need to be judged along some pre-agreed, generic dimensions such as:

- growing the business,
- reducing costs,
- developing staff.

Ideally they should be given a numerical score describing the excellence or otherwise of their performance on the specific criteria. Each employee should also agree a number of specific personal goals in the annual assessment which can be reviewed at the end of the year.

Overall, employees should be rated and told what level of performance they have achieved. Again, this would typically be:

- outstanding,
- excellent,
- acceptable,
- unacceptable.

An element of bonus, options grants, share issues and pay rise should be linked to the rating.

It is crucially important that the employee understands and accepts the rating he or she has been given. If the process throws up unresolved disagreements, employees must have a mechanism to register their disagreement in writing and to discuss their issues either with a human-relations professional or with someone else who is senior to their assessor.

Ranking

All the direct reports of the CEO (and other managers) should be ranked and can be mapped on to the sort of chart shown in Figure 6.2. This type of basic four-box matrix is a simple, shorthand way of showing where people's development needs lie.

This approach distinguishes between *performance*, which is a mixture of talent, hard work and results, and *behaviour* which is about attitude, integrity and attitudes towards others.

Obviously a CEO will hope that all their direct reports will be in the top right-hand box, but the reality is that some people will have development needs, either in terms of their skills or their style.

Some managers work hard and get great short-term financial results but 'burn-out' their workers, causing high staff turnover, or behave in ways which damage the overall image of the company. They will find themselves ranked in the top left-hand box of Figure 6.2. This group comprises people who work excessive hours

Figure 6.2   **Ranking after annual assessment**

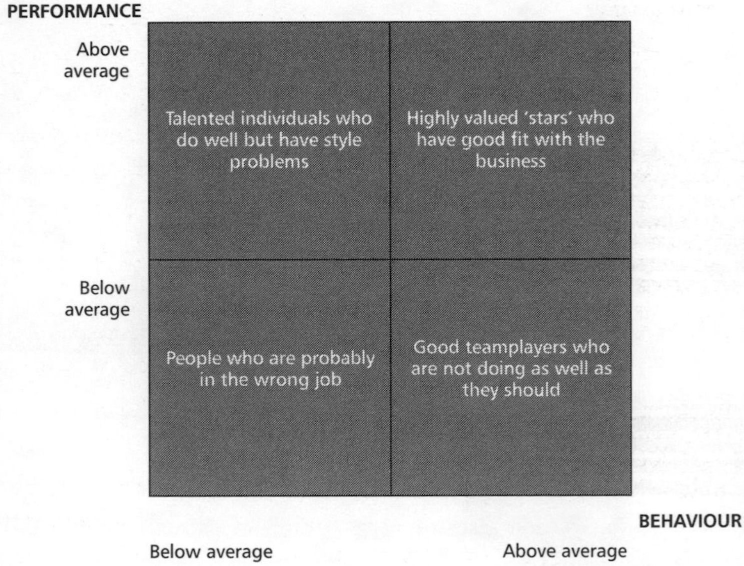

PERFORMANCE

Above average	Talented individuals who do well but have style problems	Highly valued 'stars' who have good fit with the business
Below average	People who are probably in the wrong job	Good teamplayers who are not doing as well as they should
	Below average	Above average

BEHAVIOUR

and weekends and expect their direct reports to do the same. It also includes those who slash costs and investments to hit quarterly numbers and, in doing so, damage the long-term business franchise.

People in the bottom-left box, those with bad results and a bad attitude, are very hard to deal with. These people are sometimes in breach of the psychological contract (see page 120). Those who have a good approach but are failing in their role (bottom right) need help or perhaps a different job. Figure 6.3 shows the typical action steps for people who are graded into each box.

The person being assessed should be told which box they have been placed in and why. But they must be given specific examples of what they are doing 'wrong' and told how to fix things. If you are honest with them, they can take the steps necessary to solve the

Figure 6.3   **Actions required after assessment**

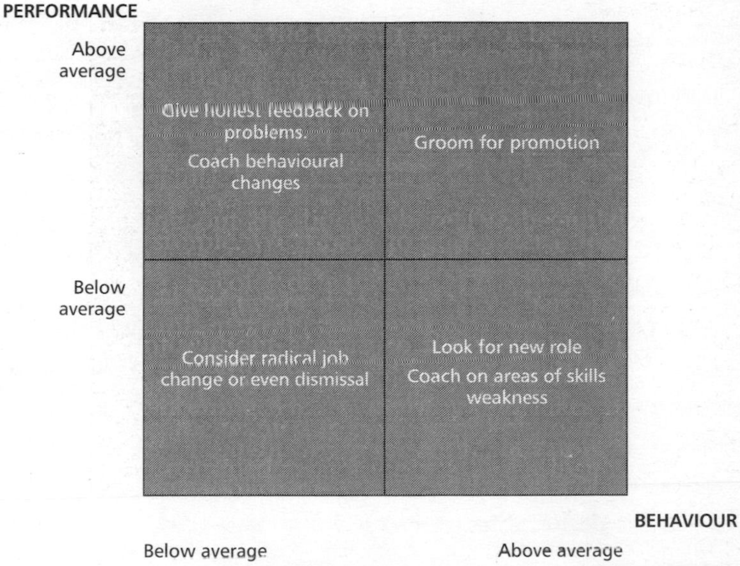

PERFORMANCE

	Below average BEHAVIOUR	Above average
Above average	Give honest feedback on problems. Coach behavioural changes	Groom for promotion
Below average	Consider radical job change or even dismissal	Look for new role Coach on areas of skills weakness

problem. People in the bottom-left box, for example, may take the initiative to seek work elsewhere. This is the correct decision for them and right for the business.

The value of feedback

In most businesses a CEO will spend dozens if not hundreds of hours a year in one-on-one conversations with their direct reports, but nearly all of these meetings will be about 'getting business done' rather than giving employment feedback. The meeting will have an agenda, a goal, a purpose which is to do with the business, not the individual. And 'social sessions' will be just that – social, with an unwritten agenda of relaxing and having fun.

The annual review falls into neither category. It is a relatively formal process with the objective of giving the direct report an opportunity for proper feedback and discussion about THEM, with the goal of two-way communication.

These reviews need to be conducted in a relaxed and business-like environment. They cannot be done on the golf course or over lunch or in the bar. By all means, buy a meal for a direct report to get to know them better but do not confuse the issue by giving them, in this social setting, formal information which has a direct bearing on their promotion prospects and compensation.

The review is an important moment in the employee's year. Diaries must be cleared for one hour or more, phones must be diverted, and the employee being assessed must be shown the same courtesy and given the same respect and time that a very senior customer would receive. For most people this one-hour annual review is the ONLY real 'what about me?' time they will get with their boss in a year and it needs to be done right.

If CEOs perform this process well with their direct reports, there is a reasonable chance the process will work all the way down the line.

Maintaining morale

Although CEOs are not, usually, directly involved with all employees, the morale of all employees is an issue the CEO should be concerned by.

To be happy, an employee needs to feel confident about a business and optimistic about the future. It is the role of all managers to keep morale high and it is the job of the CEO to help the management team achieve this. CEOs must constantly get feedback on employee issues and take steps to address concerns.

SURVIVING THE ANTARCTIC

In 1914 Sir Ernest Shackleton led an expedition of twenty-eight men with the aim of walking from one edge of the continent of Antarctica to the other. Unfortunately his ship *Endurance* became stuck in the ice and his team had to abandon it.

For many months his team walked across ice floes, undertook a dangerous sea voyage, and ended up camped on frozen, deserted Elephant Island. Shackleton and five colleagues then set off on an 800-mile journey in a small boat across the South Atlantic to seek rescue. In the end all the men lived to tell the tale. It was an epic story of survival where many other adventurers had perished.

In accounts given by the men, the thing that comes through again and again is that they owed their lives to having kept calm and kept their spirits high. Shackleton used many morale-boosting tactics and, in particular, was always outwardly cheerful and optimistic. He also made sure his men stayed busy, and kept enthusiasm high by focusing on many small, daily victories, making no promises about eventual rescue.

Summary

- Finding talent is about more than just recruiting the right people. It also means helping employees to find the best in themselves through training and coaching.
- Company image plays a big part in attracting the best candidates and helps form a positive psychological contract in their early days.
- Effective recruitment is all about fit, which means being very clear and honest about what the job entails and asking candidates the right questions.
- Reward is based on both short-term and long-term incentives, which need to be balanced. The objective is to align the interests of managers and employees with those of shareholders.
- Annual assessments are important to keep people aware of their strengths and weaknesses. They need to be carried out objectively and should provide an opportunity for two-way dialogue. The feedback must be honest.
- CEOs must take the lead in managing morale.

7

Delegating authority: tactics

*Getting things done well, execution and implementation are
what make businesses successful enterprises but CEOs cannot
take all the tactical decisions themselves. They must delegate
authority to others who can respond to day-to-day changes in
customer tastes and competitor behaviour. CEOs communicate
strategic priorities and set the right targets to influence tactics.
They must put in place the processes to monitor whether or not
the tactics are working.*

Chief executives, by definition, must be responsible for everything that happens in their business but they cannot actually do
all the work or take all the decisions themselves. The solution is tactical, it is the delegation of tasks and devolution of authority. Having
a compelling vision and a clever strategy combined with smart people in a logical structure cannot produce results unless things actually get done. Success comes from implementation and execution.

As in a military campaign, the tactics comprise hundreds and
thousands of front-line decisions taken by managers and employees
who will, or should, come up with creative and innovative solutions
to day-to-day problems and opportunities.

Some CEOs try to dominate their whole company by taking all
key decisions themselves. Others seek to avoid conflict and spend a
lot of time seeking consensus. These types are less commercially successful than those who really delegate and devolve authority to the
right people.

Being good at tactics means empowering managers and employees so they have a sense of ownership of the issues and make the day-
to-day problems their own. Constant intervention from above

through micro-management and second-guessing is the opposite of empowerment. It demotivates people and lets them off the hook for performance.

Jeff Bezos, the founder and CEO of Amazon.com, places great emphasis on individual initiative:

> Bezos [has] an obsession with innovation and disregard
> for hierarchy. One of Amazon's most prestigious in-
> house awards is called Just Do It – the winners are
> employees who do something they think will help
> Amazon *without* getting their boss's permission.[1]

From vision to strategy to tactics

If vision is the *why* and strategy the *what*, then tactics are the *how*. And of these three it is the *how* that makes the most difference between business success and failure. Effective tactics develop directly from the implementation of a well-communicated strategy consistent with a clear vision enacted by good people who understand their role.

The *vision* for a medieval monarch might have been 'we need to take over this kingdom to enlarge our country'. The *strategy* is 'we are going to seize the castles first to allow us to move our troops more freely'. An army is raised in several divisions with the right balance of highly trained infantry and cavalry – the *structure* and *people*. Then *tactics* are all about which castle to attack and when; how to scale the walls, bring down the drawbridge and dodge the boiling oil, etc. These are decisions which can be made only at the front line and in the heat of the battle by people who understand the overall plan.

In his book about turning round IBM, CEO Lou Gerstner comments:

> Execution is really the critical part of a successful
> strategy. Getting it done, getting it done right, getting it

done better than the next person is far more important than dreaming up new visions of the future. All the great companies in the world out-execute their competitors every day.[2]

Another successful turnround was that of publisher Reed Elsevier. CEO Crispin Davis commented, 'This is not a strategy story. It's about execution.'[3]

Tactics are about making things happen. It's the aspect of management where 'the rubber hits the road'. It is about getting people to understand the overall objective and to achieve the, often changing, short-term objectives. They need to feel a sense of 'it's my problem to solve'. Tactics concern the whole team.

EXPLAINING THE 'NELSON TOUCH'

The British naval hero Admiral Lord Nelson was an unconventional commander who got very much involved in the heat of battle and sustained many injuries during his career by putting himself in the front line. However, the secret of his success was his approach to delegation which, at the time, was revolutionary.

Nelson led his crews to two decisive and total victories – the Battle of the Nile (1798) and the Battle of Trafalgar (1805). This was at a time when most naval engagements simply resulted in great damage to both fleets, with no clear winner. Nelson, by contrast, destroyed the enemy conclusively.

Before both battles he invited all his ships' captains to dinner, explained exactly what he was planning to do and how each of them would be expected to take his own tactical decisions on his own initiative once the battles were started.

At the Nile some resourceful and empowered captains – acting alone – managed to get between the French ships and the land, which gave them the huge advantage of surprise and the ability to attack an undefended flank.

At Trafalgar the British astonished the French by splitting their own fleet into two lines, sailing directly at the French rather than following the more conventional 'broadside' approach. This tactic enabled Nelson's flagship *Victory* itself to unleash a bombardment which critically damaged the stem of the French flagship. Other captains also found themselves in very advantageous positions. Indeed, even after Nelson was fatally wounded early in the battle (because he was too visible on deck), his captains, knowing what was expected of them, went on to win a famous victory based on many individual acts of initiative and heroism.

In his briefing to his officers before Trafalgar, Nelson described his own approach as the 'Nelson touch'. The message being that the leadership skill was to communicate and describe the vision and the strategy and leave the tactics up to the individuals.

THE TACTICS OF MERRILL LYNCH

Merrill Lynch is one of the world's leading stockbroking firms. Charles Merrill founded it before the Second World War. The underlying concept of Merrill Lynch was to sell stock to retail customers, as opposed to what had been the normal client base of wealthy investors and institutions only.

In his biographical essay on Charles Merrill, author Daniel Gross quotes his subject explaining his vision: 'We must bring Wall Street to Main Street – and we must use the efficient mass merchandising methods of the chain store to do it.'[4]

Merrill's strategy to realise this vision was to operate a large number of branch offices across America. He achieved this partly by acquiring another broking firm, E. A. Pierce, but also by implementing an aggressive programme of office openings. By 1950 the firm had 106 offices across the USA. To execute the strategy Merrill had a series of tactics to achieve the target of recruiting new customers.[5] These included:

- Establishing a training school for war veterans in 1945 to recruit an 'army' of young retail brokers who would sell directly to the public.
- Advertising heavily to promote Merrill as a retail brand. In 1949 the firm ran more than 2,700 advertisements in more than 280 different newspapers.
- Outfitting branded buses with wireless telephones and stock market tickers (an innovation in 1954) and parking them at factories and supermarkets to sign up retail customers.
- Setting up a stock information centre in the middle of New York's Grand Central Station in 1956 to sign up passengers as clients.

It was tactics like these – all directly linked to the strategy of signing up retail customers – that led to the nickname 'The Thundering Herd' for the Merrill retail brokers and helped the firm to be the best recognised route to the stock market for the normal middle-income family.

The *vision* of widespread public share ownership was served by the *strategy* of opening retail offices and by the *tactics* of mass promotion.

Delegation, devolution and dereliction

To delegate a task means to give someone else the authority and the resources to get the job done but to accept that the ultimate responsibility lies with you. Delegation does not get you off the hook for the task, it simply means someone else is going to do it for you.

Devolution means you pass responsibility and decision making for part of the business to someone else. You will monitor performance and judge those people on results but they carry the responsibility for achieving set goals in the way they see fit. As CEO, you are still ultimately responsible, but more for the result than how it gets done.

The distinction is important. I feel you should, genuinely, devolve authority to managers running business units otherwise they cannot have the sense of autonomy and freedom they need in order to be effective. People running business units must be able to say 'it's my business'. If someone feels this ownership, they will seek solutions.

However, no commercial organisation can really thrive if the top managers and the CEO distance themselves from the performance of even the smallest part of it, and shrug, and say 'that's not my problem'. CEOs have to feel responsible for everything done in their name. Anything else is a dereliction of duty.

In their book *Execution: The Discipline of Getting Things Done* Larry Bossidy and Ram Charan make the point:

> Lots of business leaders like to think that the top dog is
> exempt from the details of actually running things. This
> is a dangerous fallacy. The leader has to be engaged
> personally and deeply in the business. There's an
> enormous difference between leading an organisation
> and presiding over it.[6]

Really impressive service businesses like Four Seasons Hotels or Avis Rent-a-Car make or break their reputations with their customers by the actions of clerks and concierges. These are the employees in the front line. I am sure the CEOs of those businesses feel they retain the *responsibility* for the service provided by junior staff, even though the actual task has been delegated through several layers.

To enable managers to make rapid and effective decisions, they need a lot of authority, but to maintain a company's performance they must also accept close financial monitoring and assessment.

In their 1980s business classic *In Search of Excellence* Tom Peters and Bob Waterman described one of the characteristics of success as 'loose–tight' management:

> Simultaneous loose–tight management practice ... is in
> essence the co-existence of firm central direction and
> maximum individual autonomy. Organisations that live

by the loose–tight principle are on the one hand rigidly controlled, yet at the same time all allow (indeed insist on) autonomy, entrepreneurship and innovation.[7]

They make the point that good control is more a matter of systems than upward referral of decisions.

A similar point was made some twenty years later in another business best-seller *Good to Great* by Jim Collins. In analysing what makes some companies great, he commented on a cultural approach to discipline as being a far more effective tool than rigid supervisory control. He described the approach at Abbott Laboratories developed by their chief finance officer:

> He [the CFO] developed a whole new framework of accounting that he called Responsibility Accounting, wherein every item of cost, income, and investment would be clearly identified with a single individual responsible for that item. The idea, radical for the 1960s, was to create a system wherein *every* Abbott manager in *every* type of job was responsible for his or her return on investment, ... Abbott recruited entrepreneurial leaders and gave them freedom to determine the best path to achieving their objectives. On the other hand individuals had to commit fully to the Abbott system and were held rigorously accountable for their objectives. They had freedom but freedom within a framework.[8]

DEVOLUTION AT GE

To be good at their job CEOs do not need to be experts in all their company's activities. In his autobiography Jack Welch commented on criticisms of him after GE acquired the television network NBC:

People would always say to me 'How can you own NBC? You don't know anything about dramas or comedies.' That's true, but I can't build a jet engine or turbine, either. My job at GE was to deal with resources – people and dollars I offered as much (or as little) help to our aircraft engine design engineers as I offered to the people picking shows in Hollywood.[9]

THE BALANCED DIET AT MCDONALD'S

The McDonald's business model is based on the idea of franchising the restaurant concept to individual operators. Founder Ray Kroc was very clear that he wanted to help his operators do well: 'My belief was I had to help the individual operator succeed in every way I could. His success would insure my success.'[10]

In an essay on McDonald's, Daniel Gross notes: 'Ray Kroc's genius was building a system that requires all of its members to follow corporate-like rules but at the same time rewards them for expressing their individual creativity.'[11] The freedom allowed to individual operators sparked creative solutions to respond to customer demand.

An operator in Pittsburgh developed the 'Big Mac' double-burger concept. The Ronald McDonald advertising character was devised by franchises in Washington DC. The Egg McMuffin and the Filet-o-Fish came from individual managers and were later offered around the group world-wide. Local franchises have the flexibility to offer local variations such as MacLak salmon fillets in Norway, McSpaghetti noodles in the Philippines and beer in Germany.

Decision-making styles
Organisations can usually be described as having one of four decision-making approaches (Figure 7.1):

Figure 7.1   **Decision-making styles**

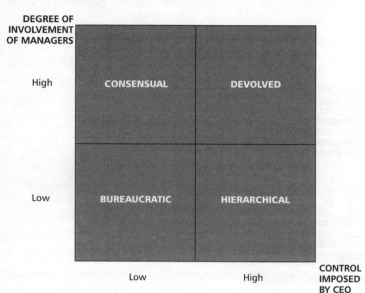

1 Hierarchical. Decisions have to be referred upwards. Managers simply carry out instructions. The CEO's word is law. Typical in France.
2 Bureaucratic. Decisions must be processed using rigorous rules. The system becomes more important than the CEO. Even the CEO finds it hard to get things done. Typical in India.
3 Consensual. Committees to achieve consensus, must discuss everything of substance. The CEO needs to be a diplomat. Typical in Japan.
4 Devolved. Individuals take real decisions but financial results are closely monitored centrally. Typical in USA and UK.

The styles that involve managers (consensual and devolved) tend to characterise companies which are good at tactics and which respond well to changes in the market. The devolved approach depends on individuals taking initiatives but requires that the CEO retains control by monitoring results.

Measurement, management and metrics

'If you cannot measure it, you cannot manage it'. It may be a familiar phrase but is none the less a very important idea. Leaders of large companies cannot possibly take all the day-to-day decisions themselves. But they can, and should, set the measures against which business performance will be judged. They must know what is going on.

Accountants are much maligned in business for carefully collecting and processing the 'wrong' information. Many CEOs complain that their accounting teams focus so much on technical definitions of profit that they fail to notice what is really happening in a business. The accountants' problem is that different people want different things.

Shareholders (the accountants' *real* clients) want to know that management are being honest with their money. They want to know what were the company's real sales. Were the costs of the business legitimate? How much did the managers pay themselves? They want simple measures such as profit, return on capital, debt ratios, etc. as they need to be able to judge one business investment against another.

Managers themselves need very different measures to tell them how they are doing with respect to customers and competitors and each other. They need information about how to make the business better.

The CEO of a company is mainly judged by the overall financial results of the company itself. However, the way for a company to achieve this success is for operating managers to focus on performance criteria other than the simple, high-level financial measures.

The balanced scorecard

In a now famous *Harvard Business Review* article Robert Kaplan and David Norton introduced the idea of the 'balanced score card'. The article starts:

> What you measure is what you get. Senior executives understand that their organisation's measurement system strongly affects the behaviour of managers and employees ... traditional financial accounting measures like ROI and EPS can give misleading signals.[12]

They go on to argue that a balanced mixture of operating measures and financial statistics produced the best results.

> Think of the balanced score card as the dials and indicators in an airplane cockpit. For the complex task of navigating and flying an airplane, pilots need detailed information about many aspects of the flight. They need information on fuel, air speed, altitude, bearing, destination, and other indicators that summarize the current and predicted environment. Reliance on one instrument can be fatal.

According to Kaplan and Norton, a company needs to have measures in place to answer four questions:

1 How do we look to shareholders? (Shareholder perspective.)
2 How do customers see us? (Customer perspective.)
3 What must we excel at? (Internal perspective.)
4 Can we continue to improve and add value? (Innovation and learning perspective.)

The shareholder perspective is largely concerned with the traditional, external financial measures but the other dimensions of success require measurement devices, many of which will be specific to a particular company in a particular industry.

Feeling the pulse of the business

All businesses have particular operating statistics or metrics which really do get to the heart of whether they are doing well or not. It is the number that really tells you if the business is healthy. It is not necessarily the annual profit, but how a company is doing along some dimension that gives insight into the effective use of its assets.

All operating managers will collect and analyse statistics important to them but it's up to the CEO to define and obtain the data that he or she really need to gauge what is happening. CEOs need to be curious and questioning to ensure their business really is looking at the right things:

- What measures are competitors using?
- What do stock market analysts look at?
- What do experienced line managers and operating people feel is a good measure?
- What do I want to know when deciding whether to reward or fire a manager?

Having established the right performance criteria, the data must be collected regularly, and analysed properly and, above all, reacted to correctly.

Key performance indicators

The operating statistics that really matter vary from business to business and are, obviously, very specific to different industries.

In many types of retailing the key measure is daily sales. These include sales per square foot or sales per salesperson. In commercial radio it is sales per minute of airtime and listening figures. Success in a restaurant is about table-turn (how many times each table gets used each day) and wastage – how much purchased and prepared food goes unsold. In newspapers it is changes in circulation and yield per advertising page.

The average occupancy of hotel rooms, the load factors in an airline (passengers per seat mile flown) or the time taken to serve a hamburger in a fast-food outlet – all these give a business specific insight. In understanding your own business you need to know the right metrics for what you do. The real insights come from measures which are specific to the business itself.

There is an increasing focus on understanding profitability by customer, with computer systems being used to collect and analyse data for all transactions between a business and its clients.

Measures that matter

When buying a company or moving to a new business it is fascinating to look at the often vast collection of monthly reports which appear in board packs and review meetings.

Over a long period of time the emphasis on what is important in any business will change. A sudden obsession with product quality will produce a slew of reports on defect levels and percentages of product returns. A consulting study about customer relationships will lead to monthly reports of customer satisfaction and complaints.

After a while so much data are being collected that senior management stop reading it all. They comfort themselves that someone must be taking an interest, as the data are collected in the first place. This is normally an erroneous belief as the data collectors do not analyse the results looking for problems, nor do they have an incentive or the power to fix things.

To be effective, people need to 'own' measures and management reports in the way general managers 'own' businesses. If, for example, low staff turnover in the sales department really is an important contributor to reduced cost and improved profitability, then someone should have the task and the financial incentive to monitor it constantly and find ways to improve it. But this does not mean a general collection of staff turnover data across the whole company is of value. If someone is not asking for and acting upon information, then do not collect it. Merely to collect information with no resulting action is costly, pointless and frustrating.

Business processes

The flip side of devolving authority and delegating tasks is that managers must adhere to rules and be active supporters of business processes that have been designed to capture and assess all the relevant management information. These provide a control environment within which managers can follow their own tactical decision-making. It is not the individual decisions that are monitored and judged, but the effect that they are having on performance.

Done well, the various business processes should be liberating, not constraining.

Business plans

Business plans are statements of aspiration and an attempt to predict the future. They help map out the shape of a business over a three- to five-year time horizon. They cannot be definitive or accurate as no one can see that far into the future with any certainty. They are a communication tool to ensure that everyone is on the same page in terms of strategy and objectives.

The process of preparing the plan forces people to think about where their business is going and should throw up any major mismatches between hopes and resources. Business plans which are full of fine detail and show cash flow three years out and to several places of decimals are classic indicators of a management that is spending too much time with its spreadsheets and not enough with its customers.

Some of the best business plans are just a few pages long but manage to highlight key issues expected to arise. The detailed projections should go into the budget which is focused on the more immediate future of the next twelve months.

Budgets that help, not hinder

The annual budget is the corporate equivalent of the regular medical check up. It is not looked forward to and there is much relief if one can leave the office without hearing any major bad news and not too many stern warnings about diet and exercise.

For many managers it is a wasted opportunity. In some companies the budget is reviled as a terrible waste of time. In others it is a complex poker game played between business unit managers and the corporate centre as the basis for bonus payments.

In an articled entitled 'Corporate Budgeting is Broken – Let's Fix It' Michael Jensen commented:

> Corporate budgeting is a joke and everyone knows it. It consumes a huge amount of executives' time, forcing them into endless rounds of dull meetings and tense negotiations. It encourages managers to lie and cheat, low-balling targets and inflating results.[13]

In his autobiography, Jack Welch describes the annual budget as 'an enervating exercise in minimalism'. He goes on to explain that GE sets stretch targets and says: 'The team knows they're going to be measured against the prior year and relative performance against competitors – not against a highly negotiated internal number.'[14]

To be effective the budget must be de-coupled from bonuses and should be an honest attempt by a management team to assess what will really happen to their business over the next twelve months and to judge what resources they will need.

Budgets are important as they provide a discipline, particularly in respect of the cost base, and they produce annual, quarterly and monthly goals against which progress can be judged. They are not absolute promises of performance.

Business review sessions

Having established some budget *goal*, which is then expressed on a monthly basis, a mechanism is required to monitor performance. Typically this takes the form of some sort of monthly report and normally a regular meeting. At this meeting the actual results compared to the same period in the prior year, and the goals in the budget, are reported. Also the pre-agreed key performance indicators are reported on and analysed.

A *forecast* of the likely financial outcome (sales, profits, cash flow) for the quarter to come and the year ahead should be revised each month. The forecast will be ahead or behind the budget goal depending on performance.

Shareholders in large public companies tend to get their news once every three months and it is purely historic, looking at past performance. Managers should get their own information, on a monthly basis at least, and should always be looking forward to the insights into future performance given by order books and predictions of customer requirements.

The monthly meeting is the process whereby CEOs can find out what is *going* to happen as well as what has actually occurred in all the business units they control. It is more than just an historic report. The monthly review is by far the most important management process as it should throw up early warnings of problems and is an excellent forum for senior managers to constantly assess performance of business unit leaders.

Board meetings

In most public companies the board meets regularly to meet its legal obligations on behalf of shareholders to monitor managerial performance. It frequently has to approve the public release of results and satisfy itself that all public statements are accurate. Far too many companies confuse the board process (which is corporate govern-ance) with the executive process (which is running the business).

The regular board is the forum for the CEO to inform directors about progress and to get their decisions on substantive investment issues. It does not run the company on a day-to-day basis.

Audit reports

The purpose of an external audit is to ensure that companies report their results correctly and that reporting is done on a basis which al-lows comparison between companies by using common standards. It is a process which looks backwards rather than forwards, and makes little or no contribution to the running of a business unless it throws up mistakes being made in the normal monthly reporting.

One of the major causes of the recent corporate scandals was that some auditors became too keen to work *with* managers to present accounts in ways that helped boost reported earnings. It seems painfully obvious that there is a conflict of interest between auditors (who adopt the role of corporate policeman) and consultants and tax-planners (who are more like corporate bandits). For one firm to provide all these services always looked like it was going to end in tears. And it did.

Spreading best practice

Another aspect of good tactics is having mechanisms in place to help a business get constantly smarter, help managers to learn from past successes and failures and make that knowledge widely available in-side the company. Such practice creates the 'learning organisation'.

In one of the most influential articles on the subject, David Garvin offers a definition: 'A learning organisation is an organisation skilled at creating, acquiring and transferring knowledge, and at modifying its behaviour to reflect new knowledge and insights.'[15]

The leader of a business has a particular role to play in best practice transfer because the CEO has an absolute right to be curious about how things work and to seek to implement ideas elsewhere. Most managers are, quite correctly, focused on getting their daily tasks done and have neither the time nor the opportunity to look around the business or to seek good ideas that might have value. It is the CEO's duty to do this.

Sharing best practice requires people to confront one of the most insidious corporate problems – the 'not invented here' syndrome. The path to making best practice transfer work is as much cultural as it is to do with systems. Good ideas and successful innovations need to be identified and described and the people behind them given visibility inside the company. The CEO and senior management need to develop a deep curiosity about ideas and then spend a lot of time telling other people about them.

When ideas are successfully adopted, the managers in charge must be rewarded and, again, their achievements communicated to others. People who are seen to take on the ideas of others must be applauded. The use of intranets – internal computer networks – is a major advance in spreading ideas and making templates of good practice available.

Brand management

A brand makes a promise to a consumer about quality and consistency. It also provides a framework to tell managers and employees how to act.

If you work as a member of staff at a Four Seasons hotel, it implies you adopt certain behaviour. Behaviour which would be very different if you worked in a $30-a night motel chain. If you are selling Johnnie Walker Black Label whisky, you would almost certainly use different distribution outlets, packaging, display and advertising than for a 'no-name' whisky. The brand provides a template for the tactics.

Many large businesses have multiple brands in addition to their own corporate brand. Successful brand management is a classic example of tactics within a strategic structure.

Some people will say that brands are far too important to be left to anyone other than the CEO. I disagree. They are too important to be taken away from the people who really control them. They are at the heart of the delegation and devolution argument. Everyone in the company must feel responsible, as they have to behave in such a way as to support the brand values.

In Chapter 1 I quoted the Unilever CEO, Niall FitzGerald, saying, 'brand reputation lies *at least as* heavily with the CEO as it does with the companies' brand managers'. The emphasis is mine. It is certainly correct that brands are of sufficient importance to a business that the CEO should worry about them and ask pointed questions if he or she suspects brand values are being compromised. But the tactics of day-to-day brand management must be left to the brand managers and marketing professionals.

To continue the Niall FitzGerald quote:

> Consumers may read disturbing reports of a company
> in the newspaper, see its trucks being badly driven on
> the motorway, be infuriated by incomprehensible
> instruction leaflets, be driven mad by the company's
> call centre, receive graceless and mis-spelt letters from
> head office. Each of these encounters has the potential
> to inflict serious harm on a brand's reputation.[16]

The CEO does not write leaflets but must take a direct interest in their quality and impact. This is why the protection of the brand must reside in all levels of the company. Everyone must be personally responsible and not feel it is all being done for them.

To anyone watching great retailers such as the late Sam Walton of Wal-Mart or Sir Stanley Kalms of Dixons inspecting their stores, it might have looked like they 'interfered' a lot. They would fret over minor details of how merchandise was presented or priced. They asked difficult questions and made suggestions. It might have driven individual store managers mad, but it led to better overall customer service. This is not micro-management but micro-observation. It is preserving brand values. The fact that store managers feel they are being checked up on by a *customer* (who happens to be their CEO), should, if it is done well, remind them that their real customers do this every day.

FOUR SEASONS' FOCUS ON SERVICE

The Four Seasons hotel group is frequently cited as the world's 'best' hotel operator. Much of the perceived excellence comes from exceptionally high levels of service. Four Seasons base their approach on getting staff to excel at solving customer problems. In a profile, *Forbes* magazine gave some examples:

> One weekend a guest realised that a mother of pearl button on the suit she intended to wear to her daughter's college graduation had broken. A hotel seamstress could not find any appropriate button in the hotel but remembered she had a similar dress at home. She called her husband who made a 45-minute bus ride so the button could be transferred and the day was saved …When guests walk down the halls hotel employees greet them heartily and step aside as they pass. On check-out guests are offered glasses of fresh lemonade or iced tea for the road.[17]

The founder of the Four Seasons, Isadore Sharpe, was quoted as

saying, 'It isn't about the amenities in the bathroom, it isn't about architecture; it's all about dealing with people in a sincere way.' The *Forbes*
profile goes on to point out that recruitment and training are the key to
getting all employees to take decisions that will help protect the brand
values.

Summary

- Actually getting things done is very difficult but is the biggest factor in determining success or failure. Tactical decisions must be left to managers and staff who are in day-to-day contact with customers and suppliers and who can respond rapidly.
- Managers will be good at tactics when they understand the big picture and their role in it, and have a sense of ownership of the problems.
- True delegation of authority is required to make managers and employees feel empowered but it must be linked to rigorous financial reporting. This is the idea of the loose–tight organisation.
- To allow managers freedom it is necessary to monitor the right management information, which gives real insight into how the business is doing. The price of autonomy is regular reporting.
- Business processes for collecting and discussing this information should be simple and should not collect information that is not used. The most important process is the monthly business review.
- CEOs must identify and spread best practice and use their leadership role to overcome the 'not invented here' syndrome.
- Management of a brand is a key part of tactics, as brand values provide guidelines for employee behaviour.

8　Operating effectively: cash

*Businesses must generate cash to justify the title 'enterprise'.
They can appear to increase sales and profits by acquisition and
by investment in new assets but the real test is growth in cash
generation. Getting cash from the business means efficient use
of the assets. This is not directly a job for the CEO but the CEO
must make it a top priority for the management team and
monitor it constantly.*

CEOs are not normally involved in the minutiae of day-to-day
operations. Their role is to get the right managers in place and
to ensure they are managing the right things. However, the CEO
should take a close interest in cash generation. As a business becomes
more complex, and individual managers more focused on their own
area of activity, there is a risk that they lose sight of the need to generate cash and become distracted chasing the wrong objectives.

Getting the right things done

As I argued in the last chapter, a compelling vision and a clear strategy will be let down by poor tactics which result in weak operations.
To be operationally effective a company must focus on generating
cash and must 'sweat' its assets to get the best out of them.

- Marketing should seek to reconfigure products and services to
  provide maximum value for customers and thus boost margins.
- Overheads have to be squeezed by eliminating unnecessary tasks.
- Working capital tied up in business is reduced by active
  management.

- Capital investment is kept to a minimum.

All this allows the generation of cash, which is the only real measure of long-term success.

Cash generation, like tactics, should be devolved to line managers and employees who are much closer to the 'action'. The role of the CEO is to take an holistic or 'total business' approach to ensure the right operational priorities are followed. However, unlike tactics, where the objective is to get all people in the business coming up with clever ways to beat the competition, operations is about the single-minded focus on cash.

To get the best from line managers they should be encouraged to focus on the narrow issues and granular details that are important in the part of the business system that they control. They should become involved in the nitty-gritty of their operation. In the same way that general managers must be encouraged to 'own' their business units, line managers and employees must 'own' various operating processes and be incentivised constantly to improve operational effectiveness.

Business as a cash machine

In simple cash terms a business is a 'black box'. Into it goes cash from issuing equity and borrowing debt. Sales of goods and services also bring in cash, as do asset sales. Inputs like labour, raw materials and energy require cash to flow out. So does the payment of tax if the company produces profits. Working capital is the cash that is 'stuck' in the business to pay for things like unsold stocks in the warehouse, work in progress and uncollected debts (Figure 8.1). At the end of the day, the business must produce more cash than it consumes or it is not going to survive.

Businesses can be making 'profits' but consuming cash which, ultimately, will cause them to fail. A classic cause of cash consumption

Figure 8.1   **Cash flow**

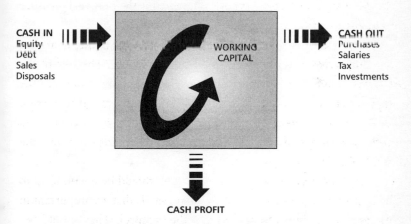

is the inability to collect actual cash from customers who are happy to buy goods and services on credit but less happy to pay for them on time. Another cash drain is repeated heavy capital investment in new plant and equipment which may generate incremental sales but which actually provides less return than the cost of borrowing the cash in the first place. CEOs obviously cannot directly control all the elements of cash generation but they must make sure they have systems in place to monitor cash and to reward managers for doing the right thing.

Figure 8.2 is a cash model for any business. The five items in the third column of Figure 8.2 provide the structure of this chapter. The CEO must ensure that all these sources/uses of cash are being monitored and managed.

Sales do not always generate cash. Left alone, a sales manager might focus too much on sales volume (which often generates maximum commission) but not be directly concerned by cash generation. They need to be measured and rewarded on improving the

Figure 8.2   **Cash generation**

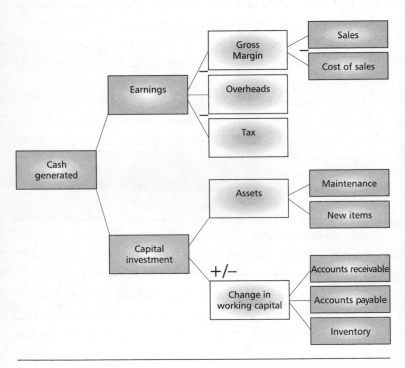

Gross Margin. Bigger margins normally produce more cash, as they reflect a higher yield from customers.

Overheads – and their control – need to be managed by the staff who are directly involved. They need to have a sense of ownership of the processes under their control and a desire to make them more efficient. No amount of consultants with clipboards can do better than an experienced and motivated foreman in improving an industrial process. Many of the initiatives are, of themselves, small scale, but hundreds of small initiatives add up to substantial improvements.

Careful *tax* planning by the CFO can reduce the amount of cash that leaks out to the government. They can also reduce the interest charges on borrowings.

Maintenance staff can often find ways to make equipment last longer without replacement, which saves capital expenditure on *assets*, which means less cash being absorbed.

Similarly, chasing late payers can reduce outstanding debts and thus also reduce the amount of cash — in this case *working capital* — tied up in the business.

Everyone in the business has a role to play in generating cash and will do so if clearly told it is the priority and if they are rewarded for their efforts.

Marketing is margin enhancing

The gross margin of a business is the difference between the income that it gets from sales and what it costs to create the products or services. It is, in a way, a measure of the value added by that business.

Typically the highest gross margins are found with new products and new technologies, for which the consumer is prepared to pay a high premium for novelty, and in which competition has not launched a price war or created a commodity product. Gross margins are also high where the product or service requires a high level of capital investment, which means that the gross margin has to cover the cost of servicing that investment.

All other things being equal, the margin will be highest when the consumer places a high value on the product or service.

Skilful marketing is a very effective margin-enhancing tool as it identifies and serves a customer need. Marketing means finding products and services that are valued by customers and providing them at the lowest possible cost to the company. Marketing is certainly not just advertising and promotion to stimulate sales. It is about really understanding consumers' needs and motivations and meeting those needs.

SALES GROWTH CAN BE COSTLY

When I was working for a communications group we purchased a small, specialist advertising agency. The agency had been growing fast and the management of the communications group felt that the managing director of the agency was something of a star with a real gift for winning business and boosting sales. He was.

Within months of buying the agency we found it was still winning new clients and getting excellent trade press coverage for its growth. The only problem was that each month it required additional cash loans from our holding company to meet its wages bill. On closer examination two things become clear.

Firstly the managing director hired top talent and was happy to pay top rates for them. This impressed clients and resulted in excellent work but the agency clients were paying the same level of commission (15 per cent of the advertising time and space purchased on their behalf) as at all other agencies. This meant that the cost of providing the client service was higher than for competitors but the income was the same. As each new piece of business was won by this high-cost 'machine' the gross margin actually went down.

Secondly a number of the clients were very slow payers. They were using the very lax cash collection of the agency to help finance their own operations. The managing director was very reluctant to get aggressive about collecting what was owed for fear of upsetting clients.

When the monthly injection of cash could go on no longer, I was asked to try to find a solution. In the end it all came down to client relationship management which, in this context, could be described as marketing.

A team from the holding company contacted all clients and explained we would have to charge a small extra fee over and above the commission to reflect the higher quality of the agency team. A number of clients complained but most were happy to pay as they valued the work. We also strictly enforced a pay-in-30 days rule, after which we charged interest. Again some clients left the agency but the others paid on time.

The net result was that the agency lost sales and went down in the trade press table but it started to generate rather than consume cash. Growth had been killing the business. The solution was to understand gross margins, not sales volumes. Getting the right customers to pay more was marketing in action.

MARGINS FROM YOGHURT

My local supermarket carries more than 100 different types of yoghurt. As a child I remember how exotic the plain white stuff seemed. At the time it commanded a high price through novelty value. Now I can get Apricot and Vanilla in light, bio and regular and with or without rice.

All these brand extensions and new varieties were not developed just for fun. They exist because the consumer is prepared to pay extra and to create new, high-margin products out of an existing commodity. The cost of ingredients, packaging and distribution is not that much more, indeed is probably less than the old plain variety, but the perceived value to the customer is greater.

Someone in the food companies is doing their research well and discovering what combination is so attractive to consumers that they are prepared to pay extra for it. Again, marketing in action.

ELECTRIC WINDOWS AS STANDARD

In the 1970s in the UK one of the hottest selling items to do-it-yourself car enthusiasts was an electric window conversion kit. British consumers were aware of this 'luxury' from America and wanted it for themselves.

Fitting electric windows as an 'add-on' extra was an expensive, time-consuming and difficult process. Conventional manufacturing wisdom was that the extra cost of electric windows as standard would deter the customer from buying the car. In fact, a factory-fitted solution was far cheaper and it worked better.

Faced with competition from Japanese car makers – who did fit at the factory – British companies started to build in the electric windows and found drivers happy to pay a premium for the product, which helped their overall margins to rise.

In retrospect it is surprising that it took so long to identify and respond to this consumer trend. But the UK car industry had a very production-led approach where engineers would decide what cars would do and customers should be grateful. Marketing skills came late.

Too much can be too much

Managers often cite high operating margins (a large difference between sales price and costs of goods) as their ultimate objective. Stock market analysts typically follow a mantra of 'high margins good, low margins bad'. This can be a dangerous delusion as the real objective is long-term cash generation and high margins may be unsustainable.

Low margins may result from a variety of factors. The most frequent assumption is that they reflect bad or lazy management. This may be the case but there are other causes. One is that a company simply has inferior economics. A retailer may have secondary, smaller sites which are less efficient; a manufacturer may have outdated, high-cost facilities which add to production costs.

Low margins may well be a competitive disadvantage if others have more effective operations. But low margins are not necessarily a bad thing in themselves. For example, high margins attract competition. Unless the barriers to entry are very substantial, competitors will be encouraged, indeed may even feel forced, to try to break into a high margin market. Very high margins usually mean someone somewhere is being squeezed. Either very tough terms are being extracted from suppliers or customers are being overcharged and/or under-serviced. In either event the situation is not stable.

MISMANAGEMENT AT MARKS & SPENCER

In her book *The Rise and Fall of Marks & Spencer* Judi Bevan notes that M&S had, at its peak in the late 1990s, a return on sales margin of 14 per cent, the highest of any retailer in the UK. But they wanted to push it further:

> At its simplest they pushed the business too hard ... They increased floor space faster than increasing employment levels ...

> The result was a theoretically more productive workforce – but in practice one that was increasingly alienated and discontented. A MORI survey showed 89 per cent of the British public trusted M&S in 1995, by 1999 that figure had fallen to 61 per cent ...

> The brand was on the skids. [She quotes an employee] 'They cut costs, cut costs and cut costs and put up prices, put up prices, put up prices'.[1]

Marks & Spencer suffered a dramatic decline in reputation, sales and profits and much of the problem could be blamed on being too aggressive with margins and not re-investing enough in preserving their brand franchise.

It's a matter of getting the balance right and CEOs must be satisfied that high margins are sustainable and that customers are not being short-changed or business resources overstretched.

Overheads: cost-cutting programmes

Overheads – at the simplest – are what a company spends on being in business. They are what it costs to run the company over and above the direct costs of buying the inputs to make its products and services.

Over time organisations can develop large numbers of unnecessary activities without knowing why they do them. Monthly statistical analyses, extra personnel reviews, coordination meetings, etc. often continue long after their raison d'être has disappeared. For instance, large teams of marketing and human resources staff are often amassed in response to a problem but are not disbanded after the problem is solved.

Preparing regular reports can consume a lot of management time and, when there are enough of them, lead to unnecessary job positions as staff have to be employed to crunch all the numbers.

When a company calls in consultants to help cut costs a standard technique is to undertake a process that looks at all the tasks being done by central staff and ask if those tasks are really of any value.

Self analysis

When I was a newly minted consultant at McKinsey we were taught a simple but very effective cost reduction technique.

Organisations were persuaded to look inwards (via a team of managers led and assisted by McKinsey consultants) and identify all the tasks that they did and analyse if they added value to the objectives of the company. Internal management reports, economics departments, brochures and showrooms were typical costs which could be eliminated. Things that had started many years ago when they had real value but were somehow just continued without question.

The reason the process worked so well is that managers themselves were asked to identify unnecessary tasks and people derived considerable satisfaction from doing away with activities which could be shown to have no benefits. They had ownership of their own business processes.

THE CHAIRMAN'S RICE PUDDING

One of my cost saving clients was a large, traditional British bank. Our investigations revealed it operated seven layers of internal employee catering from the chairman's dining room to the messengers' canteen. Each had its own catering staff and each its own menus, culture and approach.

It was quickly agreed that many of these food facilities could be dispensed with and in trying to work out which to keep, we got into more detail. Part of this was to analyse what was eaten in each of the seven layers. We saved the best for last and found ourselves in the chairman's dining room.

A heavy printed card carried that day's menu, which ended with a choice of sweets including rice pudding. Not surprisingly, as diet- and calorie-conscious consultants, we eschewed the classic school-food dessert. However, over coffee, out of curiosity, we asked to see the previous week's menu cards. Each had different, mouth-watering hors d'oeuvres and main courses on offer but each featured rice pudding.

When asked, the chef explained that he cooked not one but two rice puddings every day and that almost every day they were thrown away uneaten. When asked why, he did not know, saying it was 'tradition'. It took some days to discover that a chairman in the 1950s had been very fond of rice pudding (it probably helped to soak up the gin, wine and port that would then have been a regular feature of banking lunches) and had requested it every day. No one had thought to countermand the order. It took an active intervention to stop it. The same is true of many management practices.

THE MESSENGER RUN

The same bank had its own full-time staff of twelve messengers in central London, mostly ex-army, whose task it was (when not eating in their own canteen) to take packages and documents between bank branches, and to and from other offices such as the Bank of England, and those of lawyers and accountants.

Every day there were five 'runs' scheduled between the bank's main London offices. The boxes for first run at 8.30am were always full from the previous night or with overnight communications from the USA and Asia. The last run of the day also featured full boxes.

In a classic piece of junior consultants' analysis we tracked the volume of the boxes in each run over a two-week period. We found that 80 per cent of the paper went in the first and last runs of the day and that, on some occasions, the 11am boxes were actually completely empty. A real-life example of the Pareto principle (page 83).

It was surprising how many managers defended the messenger service as a key part of the bank's infrastructure, a valuable tradition, a security benefit and just a 'nice thing to have', but after some pressure from the CEO the messenger staff was cut back to four and the number of daily runs reduced. Documents still moved around without problems and the messengers' canteen got closed.

CHAINSAW AL – A CUT TOO FAR

Cutting back genuinely redundant overheads, which are simply a hang-over from history, is one thing – making a career out of being a cost cutter is another.

In July 1996 when Al Dunlap arrived at Sunbeam – a manufacturer of small domestic appliances like electric blankets and toasters – the stock price jumped by 50 per cent in anticipation of his ruthless cost-cutting approach that had been successful at other companies. Within four months Dunlap had announced the closure or sale of twelve of Sunbeam's eighteen plants and the firing of around half of its 12,000 employees. He was living up to his nickname of 'Chainsaw Al'.

For 1997 the company reported record sales and earnings but by early 1998 the company was reporting big losses. The share price collapsed, and there were a further 5,000 job losses. The business had been de-stroyed by ill-considered cuts. In June 1998 the board fired Dunlap be-cause, they said, 'he couldn't make his own numbers'.[2]

You cannot cut your way to success. Overhead cuts only work when they genuinely reflect the abolition of unnecessary activities. Cuts which change the business's value proposition or reduce its control ability below acceptable levels are counter-productive. A challenge for the CEO is to ensure that the management team are not so enthusiastic about short-term cuts that they damage the long-term business.

Tax

The New York property widow Leona Helmsley famously and very unwisely said 'Only the little people pay taxes.' In a corporate con-text only those with poor finance staff pay *all* the tax they might have to on the exact timetable initially requested by the authorities.

A legitimate attempt to minimise cash outflow to the tax authori-ties is a complex and, for some, enjoyable intellectual tournament to find the best possible interpretation of the tax laws and make the maximum possible use of available allowances.

In the corporate world, as in the personal one, it is very difficult legally to avoid paying tax but it is relatively easy to defer it in many ways which, if cash generation is the key objective, might be highly desirable. The exact mechanisms vary by national tax regime and from company to company but most are based on ideas such as agreeing rapid depreciation of assets, borrowing large sums to make the interest tax deductible, generating profits in low-tax areas and charging corporate costs in high-tax areas.

CEOs do not need to be tax experts themselves but they do need to recognise the value of good tax work to give the company maxi-mum access to cash resources. Their chief financial officers need to be confident that the structures are as tax efficient as possible as it is

unlikely that most line managers will give this issue more than a passing thought.

Tax planning is a source of competitive advantage and cash. Lou
Gerstner, the CEO of IBM commented:

> When I arrived, IBM was paying a huge tax bill every
> year. Over an eight-year period, we brought the tax rate
> down. That's as much a responsibility of management
> as bringing down the cost of information technology,
> real estate, and anything else. It's an expense of
> running the business.[3]

Assets

All businesses have assets for use in producing products and services.
The self-employed artist needs brushes and something to hold the
canvas. A power utility company needs a complex generation plant.

All assets wear out and require maintenance and, probably, need
replacement. The depreciation charge that appears in a company's
accounts each year is the theoretical annual cost of the assets deteri-
orating. The actual cost of keeping the assets working is a matter of
management.

There is an accounting argument about whether maintenance
costs are really capital investment or overheads, but for this purpose
it does not matter. Either involves the spending of cash to keep those
assets usable.

Depreciation DOES matter

In the 1990s it became fashionable to say that depreciation was not
an important issue. Chief executives were counselled to ignore depreciation and simply 'leave it to the accountants'. Businesses were
judged and evaluated on their EBITDA (Earnings Before Interest,
Tax, *Depreciation* and Amortisation). Depreciation was dismissed by

many analysts and investment bankers as a 'non-cash charge'. This meant that although it did figure in calculating a company's reported profits, it somehow did not affect a company's 'true' performance.

If a plumber buys a van to get from job to job he will probably purchase it for cash – say £15,000 – and in the books of his company he will show an annual depreciation charge of say £3,000. This is based on the purely theoretical assumptions that the van's useful life is five years and after five years he will need to buy a new one and the old one has zero value. These assumptions are almost bound to be wrong, but that's the way depreciation works. It is certainly true that after the initial purchase there is no cash going out but when a new van is really required – as the old one has actually gone to the scrap yard – then the plumber will have to find the cash or his business will collapse.

The same logic follows for even the largest and most complex company.

Many companies follow the rule that annual cash investment in maintenance and replacement should be equal to the depreciation charge. In effect, they are saying that depreciation is not just a theoretical concept but reflects a business reality of needing to keep assets working. This approach has the great merit of automatically keeping plant and equipment up to date but may result in investment when not strictly necessary.

Corporate raiders and leveraged buy-out firms will often acquire a company with the intention of cutting or freezing annual maintenance on the basis that this liberates cash which can be used to service and pay down debt. Over a short period of time this approach can be successful but in the end a business will usually suffer. Underinvestment usually makes a business less efficient and its products or services less attractive.

On the other hand, if a business is spending more than annual depreciation on maintenance and new items it must be able to point to growing sales and/or improving margins to justify the investment. It must show the new cash investment is being put to good use.

There is no simple formula, but CEOs need a mechanism for getting the balance right.

Corporate cost shuffling

An entire industry of specialised accounting has grown up around methods of moving business costs between the balance sheet and the profit and loss account.

At times when it is felt the profits need to look good (perhaps to hit bonus targets), costs can be capitalised – that is, designated as capital expenditure and placed on the balance sheet to be reflected later by a depreciation charge. At times when it is felt that annual cash generation and net bank debts are important then big assets can be leased in ways that incur annual rental costs rather than capital expenditure.

The best solution is simply to view both types of spending – balance sheet and profit and loss account – as a cash cost to the business.

Preventative maintenance

One of the scandals of public life in the UK is the poor and declining state of the railway network, which for decades has suffered from under-investment.

Successive governments and railway operators have simply been living off the efforts of earlier generations as tracks, signals, stations and rolling stock have become less effective. Had the railway system been a normal company in an open, competitive environment, it would have been bankrupted and closed long ago without adequate investment.

There is a tremendous temptation to under-invest to boost short-term cash. There are examples in consumer goods companies where marketing, advertising and product development costs have been slashed. Sales have held up, for a time, but over a period a brand has died and shareholder value has been lost. The short-term/long-term trade-off in respect of maintenance investment is a classic policy for a CEO to manage.

Automation and other trade-offs

Investment in new technology, IT and machinery often leads, or is intended to lead, to improved labour productivity and efficiency. All such projects need to be convincing in terms of cash payback. Managers seem oblivious to the importance of cash and happily support new investments which, when looked at critically, simply do not produce acceptable returns.

Outsourcing is another cash-generation technique as it, in effect, means making use of someone else's assets and thus not having to carry those assets on your books. You have to pay them a profit margin for doing whatever it is they do for you but if they are making use of marginal capacity their costs may be much lower than yours.

Making working capital work harder

One of the most valuable cash hoards in many businesses is tied up in its working capital: the cash needed to finance work in progress. Managers become so used to routines and process that they often fail to question whether a different approach would be more effective. CEOs need to be very inquisitive about the way working capital is used.

Many of the management techniques of the 1990s were addressed to improving practice in this area and much of the effort in techniques like business process re-design, product and process re-engineering are linked to reducing working capital.

Having twenty-five varieties of electric kettle on the shelves of your department store may give a wonderful impression of consumer choice but will bankrupt you if your competitors stock only two brands and are still able to sell twice as many by offering lower prices.

NOT SO SHARP AT GILLETTE

The consumer goods company Gillette, which is the world's leading razor maker, got itself into deep financial trouble in the closing years of the last century, losing market share and sales and building up debts. A lack of operating discipline resulted in it having far too many product varieties which sat in warehouses and storerooms. At one point they had 24,000 different SKUs (stock keeping units) which led to huge complexity and tied up enormous amounts of cash. Gillette's working capital as a percentage of sales reached a huge 36 per cent compared with less than 3 per cent for typical competitors. (Proctor & Gamble is 1 per cent and Colgate is 2.5 per cent.) Jim Kilts, the new CEO who was brought in to turn the company round, made fixing this complexity a top priority.[4]

Just-in-time

One of the simplest ways to reduce working capital is to make products to order just before they are due for delivery. This way neither finished products nor component parts are being stored at the expense of your business.

The ideal way to fulfil a customer's order is to make the product immediately the order is received and to be paid at the same time. In some ways this is what happens in a restaurant, where much of the value added is in the cooking and the presentation. But of course they do have to keep stocks of the raw materials – the food and wine – and pay rent on their buildings.

Just-in-time production is the idea of arranging the business process so that large inventories of finished or partly finished goods are not required. In industries where prices are falling – like computers – there is the added advantage that keeping a small stock reduces the write-down of inventory that would be required each year if finished goods had seen a decline in their retail value since manufacture.

THE MAGIC OF DELL

The Austin, Texas-based computer maker Dell takes customer orders by telephone and via the internet, then assembles each computer with the exact customer-defined configuration and finally ships them directly. This results in very effective management of working capital. In his book *Direct from Dell* Michael Dell explains:

> From the start our entire business – from design to manufacturing to sale – was oriented around listening to the customer, responding to the customer and delivering what the customer wanted ... While other companies had to guess which products their customers wanted, because they built them in advance of taking the order, we *knew* – because our customers told us *before* we built the product ... Other companies had to maintain high levels of inventory to stock the reseller and retail channels. Because we built only what our customers wanted, when they wanted it, we didn't have a lot of inventory taking up space and soaking up capital.[5]

The Dell business model overcomes the traditional manufacturer to wholesaler to retailer to customer chain, which is both slow and deprives the manufacturer of the knowledge of what the customer really wants.

THE GENIUS OF CARREFOUR

Even better than low working capital is negative working capital, where your customers pay you before you pay your suppliers.

Some food retailers like Carrefour and Wal-Mart will be able to nego-tiate credit terms with wholesalers and food manufactures of 30 days or more, but the products are shipped and sold to customers for cash in far less time than this.

Carrefour and other food retailers are getting what amounts to a loan from their suppliers because of their terms of trade. The same principle applies in other areas of retail but companies need excellent logistics to capture the benefits. It the same principle that made the American Ex-press travellers' cheques described in chapter 1 so profitable.

Product and process improvement

Whilst not strictly about working capital, improving efficiency in these two areas has the same effect of liberating cash. Products absorb more cash than necessary if they fail to make use of new technologies or new materials or if they are 'over-engineered' – that is if they do things that the consumer does not want to pay for. Designers must be constantly monitoring new technologies and competitor solutions to look for ways of delivering the same (or better) products at lower costs.

A production process absorbs cash if it is too slow or if it makes inefficient use of labour. It is on this area that various management concepts focus, concepts such as Six Sigma which seeks to reduce product faults; the Japanese idea of *kaizen*, which is about continuous improvement in operating practices; quality circles and business process re-engineering.

Summary

- Businesses are simple cash machines. Five key elements of the business should be monitored and assessed in terms of cash generation.
- Marketing is used to increase margins and generate more cash from the same assets.

- Overhead cuts reduce cash-draining activities.
- Tax planning reduces or delays cash outflow.
- Assets are a real cash cost to a business. Cash is consumed to buy, replace and repair them. Assets should be kept to a minimum.
- Working capital can absorb cash. Techniques like just-in-time manufacturing greatly reduce the cash tied up in the business.
- CEOs must balance the temptation to generate cash by short-term measures with the long-term creation of shareholder value.

9   Moving forward: change

Organisations do not like change, neither do individuals. An organisation, and the people in it, naturally favours the status quo. Left alone, nothing new will happen and the business will stagnate. But change is inevitable and responding to it is a crucial feature of corporate success. The CEO must lead a process of constant change and overcome the fear and resistance of the organisation and its people.

Change has become a constant; managing it has become an expanding discipline. The way we embrace it defines our future.[1]

This forward-looking sentiment comes from a surprising source. It was said by one of the world's most successful and most long-tenured leaders, Her Majesty Queen Elizabeth II, in a speech to the British Parliament to mark her Golden Jubilee in April 2002.

The Queen, who has run the British monarchy for more than fifty years, is often characterised as deeply conservative and she was well into her seventies when she made the remark. However the House of Windsor has survived and even thrived through quite extraordinary social change. At a minimum, the comment shows the boss of 'UK plc' has the leadership skills to employ excellent advisers and speechwriters.

Most of us, however, do not embrace change. We fear it and fight against it. Given that the business environment is in a constant state of flux it is amazing that companies exhibit such inertia and that management has such a strong natural propensity to keep things the way they are. Failure to change is one of the main reasons that a company declines.

It is the CEO, more than any other individual, who must initiate change and persuade reluctant and, at times, resistant colleagues to implement it. Change management is a key skill that marks out good CEOs from bad ones.

Companies have to metamorphose to outperform their peers and respond to new customer demands. Those which simply stand still will see their sales taken by competitors, their profits eroded by outdated working practices, and will find themselves slipping down the league tables of corporate performance. In the case of an hereditary monarchy, history suggests those who don't move with the times lose more than just their stock market rating.

As individuals we all understand the argument that change must happen. We can see that, for human beings, it is an inevitable, physical process. It is a necessary part of growing up: a central feature of life. But for the most part, as individuals, we do not like alterations in our work or environment. At a surprisingly young age we become creatures of habit. We are unwilling to confront and deal with new ways of doing things. Change feels risky. Routine and repetition are comforting.

Thus, for an organisation – a collection of individuals – change is also threatening and unwelcome. Change takes a company into the unknown.

Most organisational changes we experience are not major strategic shifts. They are relatively minor but they often feel highly disruptive. It can be something like altering the approved spreadsheet programme from Lotus to Excel, moving the year-end from June to December. Or moving the head office from one building to another. These types of change can be controversial and have a far-reaching effect on an individual but are not a radical change in the organisation itself.

Taking a company from publishing local newspapers in Australia to being the world's largest supplier of satellite television (News Corporation) or converting a water utility into a global film and music company (Vivendi Universal) or repositioning a manufacturer of rubber boots to become the world's largest mobile phone maker (Nokia) is macro change requiring new skills, new people and a new approach. In each case the change was defined and led by an individual. The CEO. Two of them, Rupert Murdoch of News Corporation and Jorma Ollila of Nokia, have been pretty successful. Jean-Marie Messier of Vivendi made a hash of it and lost his job.

Change is not always successful, nor is it always a 'good thing'. If it is simply done for the sake of it without clear goals and timetable, it can be damaging and expensive. Change may be imposed on a company from within as it moves to identify new opportunities or, more likely, to diversify away from what it sees as bad businesses. Or it may be forced upon it from outside by new technologies, new competitors and shifts in consumer tastes.

The American auto industry, confronted by well-engineered, low-cost Japanese cars, re-invented itself with, amongst other things, the mini-van and the SUV. The cinema industry faced with the arrival of television re-invented itself with multiplexes. The arrival of the internet and online retailing appeared to threaten a range of conventional retailers but many, after a year or two of panic, have embraced the digital world and gone online themselves with great success.

Change to a business is self-renewal. Making it happen is often the difference between corporate life and death. But it will be resisted. Not just by people inside the business but often by suppliers, customers and regulators who mistrust anything new. Because organisational change does not happen naturally it is something that the CEO must impose. If the CEO does not do it, it is unlikely anyone else will. Most managers and employees will opt for the status quo.

When I joined the consulting firm McKinsey & Co. I found that one of the first things they sent you on was an internal training programme at which they posed the question, 'What do consultants do?'. Most of the 'experienced hires' like me (those new recruits who had had a management job before) suggested things like, 'Help cut costs', 'Define strategy', 'Develop marketing plans'. The MBA graduate hires (fresh from business school) almost as one answered, 'Make change happen'.

I remember at the time being irritated by their pat responses but subsequent experience suggests that they were quite right and in fact change management is one of the most valuable roles of external consultants. Indeed, it is one of the areas where they unambiguously are worth the money.

Organisations, even those led by dynamic and open-minded CEOs, find substantial change almost impossible to impose upon themselves. There are simply too many preconceived notions and too many personal agendas. A change project will need a dedicated, full-time, internal team and will often have to bring in outsiders to provide both energy and resources. A true *enterprise* is constantly changing.

Why people resist change

In an organisation, resistance to the implementation of new ideas is easy to explain. Organisations are made up of people and most people suspect that change in their company will not, on balance, be good for them.

- 'The new set up will mean more work.'
- 'The new approach may make my bonus more difficult to earn.'
- 'The new systems will be confusing and hard to follow.'
- 'My desk will be further away from the coffee machine.'

It is very hard for individuals to accept that, at the macro level, an organisation MUST change, which will inevitably mean their own micro-level routine must alter as well.

People often resist change because they do not understand exactly what it will mean for them. This usually represents a failure of top management and, therefore, of the CEO to find compelling arguments and easy-to-understand explanations. If you go to an employee and say, ' I am going to change your contract', he or she will always ask, 'Is the change going to be to my benefit?' If the answer is 'No', you will probably be dealing with a lawyer or facing union demands for consultation.

People regard employment contracts (if they have them) as the position from which they will not retreat. If any changes do happen, they must be positive ones. New terms must be *better* than the old. They expect salaries to go up, bonuses to become easier to earn, working hours to reduce and perks to be improved. People have a legal basis for their employment and compensation. Why should they accept any deterioration?

The same is true for the non-legal contract – the *psychological contract* – between employee and employer. This unwritten deal covers areas such as: 'How am I treated by my boss?' 'How much flexibility do I have in my job?' 'Do I feel valued?' 'Is the output of my work ethical and useful?' 'Is my office comfortable and prestigious?'

The prospect of change may have an impact on the psychological deal. Again people, not unreasonably, expect change to make things better. If they have any doubts, they will resist. And they usually do have doubts.

Imagine this speech from a CEO to all employees:

> As you know, market conditions are tough. Our
> competitors have become more aggressive. Interest
> rates are rising. Our last reported profits are down.
> Shareholders are unhappy and our bankers are asking
> difficult questions. To correct these problems we are
> embarking on a major change programme with new
> remuneration structures and we'll be asking each of
> you to play your part.

Interpretation – if I was sitting in the third row:

> We are going to slash costs, which means you are either
> going to be fired or asked to work harder for less pay.

And we wonder why people resist change.

A better way to get people engaged and positive might be along the lines of:

> We have an opportunity to improve bonus plans by
> working together to improve profits. As you will know,
> the market is tough right now and our recent financial
> results have been poor. But we want to prepare
> ourselves for the upturn that will come. That means
> streamlining our business to produce higher margins.
> We are introducing new profit-sharing plans that will
> enable you to benefit from the improved performance
> that you are going to achieve.

There has to be a real incentive for individuals for them to want to support new ideas.

Stephen Friedman, who led a huge change programme at the investment bank Goldman Sachs & Co., described the change-resistant personalities:

> You have Barons, who perceive change as a risk to
> their fiefdoms and personal importance. You have
> Creationists, who feel comfortable with things as they
> are and distrust evolution. And you have Romantics,
> who hark back to some imagined Camelot, when
> every subject in the kingdom was happy and
> prosperous.[2]

Lou Gerstner, who led the turn round of IBM, also emphasises the challenges:

> Frankly if I could have chosen not to tackle the IBM
> culture head-on I probably wouldn't have. Changing
> the attitude and behaviour of hundreds of thousands of
> people is very, very hard to accomplish. Business
> schools don't teach you how to do it. You can't lead the
> revolution from the splendid isolation of corporate
> headquarters. You can't simply give a few speeches or
> write a new credo for the company and declare that the
> new culture has taken hold.[3]

The urge to sustain the status quo is deep seated. Change is hard work.

CEOs must lead change

Companies and their people need to go from here to there and from now to then. The CEO's role is to show them the way and lead them on the route.

Leading change is one of the things that make the CEO's job different from most other managers'. Most managers will spend part of their time implementing changes in their own area but the CEO must constantly impose change on the whole business. It comes back to the need for CEOs to be curious and questioning about their business.

- Do we make the right products?
- Do we have the right people?
- Where should we be in five years' time?

The answers to these questions are likely to require the development of a different type of company from the present one.

Line managers of parts of a business quite rightly worry about their own specific issues and often cannot see the wood for the trees. Indeed, to be effective, they need to focus on the details of grain and bark rather than the lie of the forest. A successful change programme must been seen to have the full commitment of the top management team. Then the line managers and others will feel more confident implementing their bits of the programme.

Change means a lot more than simply cutting costs. One of the leading change gurus, Rosabeth Moss Kanter, comments:

> Turnaround chief executives who come in to cut costs
> but who don't rethink the business model or
> assumptions are making cosmetic change: they don't
> last. But if they rethink traditional practices, challenge
> underlying business assumptions, they create
> sustainable change. Of course systemic change takes
> longer.[4]

There are many books on change management. Three of the best known are *Real Change Leaders* by Jon R. Katzenbach; *Reengineering the Corporation* by James Champy and Michael Hammer and *A Force for Change* by John P. Kotter. There are also innumerable articles. Most management consultancies have change management practices and manuals. Some *only* do change management work.

Many of the fashionable business tools of the 1980s and 1990s were linked to change. They include time based competition, just-in-time delivery, total quality management and re-engineering.

Although the process of change is ongoing, major initiatives will often be organised as a specific project. I have no perfect answer for how to do this but Figure 9.1 shows an approach that has worked for me. The key elements of a change management programme are described below.

Figure 9.1   **Change management**

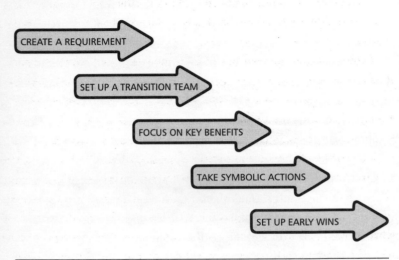

Create a requirement for change

To get people to move they have to be convinced that where they are is not a good place to be and somewhere else is better.

If a company finds itself in a true crisis, days away from bankruptcy or on the verge of losing a major contract, then it is relatively easy to persuade people that something must be done differently. But most corporate change is not like that. Often things are going just fine and it is simply that the CEO can see that problems will arise because of what is happening around them.

The CEO who does not create a 'felt need' may end up like the subaltern in the famous First World War cartoon bravely going 'over the top' with whistle in one hand and revolver in the other, only to look back to see the troops still playing cards in the trench. Change consultant Dan Cohen writes:

> It's a very common mistake. Executives come in and
> say 'Here's my vision, let's go forward.' But they fail to

create any sense of urgency about why change is
required. In other words, they don't lay the
groundwork to allow the change to take root.[5]

If you want to move your business on and you do not have a crisis,
then create one.

- Share bad news on the sales front.
- Show market research that criticises your products.
- Tell your people about the success of competitors.
- Circulate negative analysts' briefings and press reports.

In short, frighten people out of their comfort zone. Paint a picture of
what will happen if things stay as they are. Show how competitors
will take share. Explain how new technology might make products
and services redundant. Demonstrate that rising costs will wipe out
bonuses and profit sharing. Try to remove complacency and get people fired up about finding a new way.

Alan 'A.G.' Lafley, the CEO of consumer goods giant Procter &
Gamble, who is credited with leading a dramatic turn-around programme commented: 'The fact we were in a crisis made it easier to
make changes. In a crisis people accept change faster.'[6] IBM's Lou
Gerstner shares this view: 'The sine qua non of any successful
corporate transformation is public acknowledgement of the existence of a crisis. If employees do not believe a crisis exists, they will
not make the sacrifices that are necessary to change.'[7]

A WAKE-UP CALL AT XEROX

The Xerox Corporation – famous mainly for its copying machines – was
pushed close to bankruptcy in 2000 following a series of failed change
initiatives resulting in losses and high debts. The CEO was fired and
longtime Xerox manager Anne Mulcahy was given the task of saving the

company. Xerox was notoriously conservative and clung to outdated practices.

Mulcahy undertook a 90-day investigation and came up with a very radical plan to reduce overheads by $1 billion, slim down the business and sell assets. Her challenge was to get buy-in from other Xerox managers, which might have been difficult as many would have assumed that as an 'insider' she would have favoured the status quo. She explained: 'The crisis was pretty critical. I used it as a vehicle to get things done that wouldn't have been possible in times of business as usual.'[8]

In the event Mulcahy cut more than 20,000 jobs but retained the support of the company's staff. She argued her twenty-five years of working with Xerox actually helped her to be radical:

> I don't think it's a question of insider versus outsider. It's a question of leadership. All cultures need to change. Standing still is not acceptable for any company ... But I do feel strongly that you have to bring a culture with you. One of the errors is that people think you have to really fight a culture to enable change. I believe you have to motivate a culture to change.[9]

Set up a transition team

CEOs must lead change, but they cannot make it happen by themselves. People at every level in the organisation must become active and vocal supporters. The best way to do this is to establish a change team. For some of these team members it may be a full-time job. For others it should be seen as a mark of the organisation holding them in high esteem. The team is also a good mechanism for bringing in outside consulting help and creating cross-discipline and cross-divisional bonds.

The team should include managers who are well thought of and well respected and who are felt to have a 'big future' in a company. This will help win support for the programme.

Although the overall change might have been initiated and certainly visibly endorsed by the CEO, the active work needs to be delegated and assigned to create change champions throughout the business. Components of a typical change programme include:

- Implementing a new brand identity.
- Outsourcing the IT function.
- Reducing customer query response times by 25 per cent.
- Integrating three back-offices into one.

All of these are tasks which can be given to an individual or a small team. Each team implements their own changes. Added all together, they will change the whole organisation.

The team needs dedicated resources such as secretarial and visual aids support. It should have a physical place to meet – a sort of 'war room'.

There are occasions when resistance to new ideas at a senior level seems insurmountable and the CEO will go directly to the people at the front line in order to implement a programme. It is important to involve people who are real sources of influence inside the organisation.

IDENTIFY WHO CAN GET THINGS DONE

In his inspiring book *A Long Walk to Freedom* Nelson Mandela recounts his philosophy of how he learned to deal with prison authorities during nearly thirty years of captivity.

> The most important person in any prisoner's life is not the
> minister of justice, not the commissioner of prisons, not
> even the head of prison, but the warder in one's section. If

> you are cold and want an extra blanket you might petition
> the minister of justice, but you will get no response. If you
> go to the commissioner for prisons, he will say, 'Sorry, it is
> against regulations.' The head of the prison will say, 'If I
> give you an extra blanket, I must give one to everyone.' But
> if you approach the warder in your corridor, and you are on
> good terms with him, he will simply go to the stockroom
> and fetch a blanket.[10]

It is the same lesson that reminds us that being friends with the airline check-in clerk is more likely to get you a last-minute upgrade than playing golf with the airline's CEO. Organisations are made up of people.

In managing a successful change programme a CEO must win over many people at the front line of a business who, for simple practical reasons, cannot be met face to face, let alone made personal friends. Just issuing instructions for change via the line management structure is not going to win converts. CEOs have to use communications tools to recruit supporters at every level.

ORGANISED ANARCHY AT ASDA

One of the most impressive change stories of recent years was the British supermarket ASDA, which had been losing market share and was deeply troubled financially. Archie Norman and Allan Leighton were hired to implement a huge change programme which was focused on a fundamental redesign of the stores but which faced resistance.

The two men soon realised that few, if any, of the managers were willing to back their ideas. Instead of working through those managers, they struck a working alliance with store-level employees and, in so doing, deliberately undermined ASDA's existing chain of command.[11]

Allan Leighton, who went on to become chairman of Royal Mail, comments:

I've always been in companies where I've had to manage
thousands of people. I don't manage the top management
team. I think I'm responsible for everybody ... The
difference between the average and the excellent manager
is that the great managers get things done through other
people, willingly and well.[12]

Focus on key benefits

Trying to do too much too quickly will lead to initiative overload and
often bring down the whole change programme. The organisation
must be focused on a few key positive changes which will make it
easier to measure outcomes and report results.

In earlier chapters I described the CEO's role in developing vision, strategy and structure. This is even more important in a change
programme where the organisation must be given a clear, unambiguous and exciting picture of where it is going and why. Deciding a
compelling outcome makes the pain of the change process worth
putting up with.

It is not convincing just to say 'we are going to be better'. Any
statement must be specific. People must be given a reason for em-
barking on new practices:

- 'Improving meal-serving times will allow us to deal with more
  customers each day and increase our profits and bonuses.'
- 'Reducing product faults will reduce the number of returns to
  the factory, which will decrease our costs as well as improving
  our product reputation.'
- 'We will answer all incoming phone calls in ten seconds or less,
  which means we will lose fewer orders as people are less likely to
  hang up and call a competitor.'

The process must also show that the outcome of change will have specific benefits for the individual. The change management teams must work through the various scenarios in great detail so that individuals can relate to what it all means for them. The plan needs to describe basic things like the impact on office space, working hours, overtime, bonus plans and career prospects. It needs to show individuals that there is nothing to be afraid of and that the overall result should be good for them *as individuals*.

Whilst it is helpful to explain to people how the change programme will benefit the company, it is the perceived impact on *them* which will really condition their behaviour. To get individuals excited, the payment systems need to be changed to reward the new style of behaviour required.

BACK TO BASICS AT P&G

Procter & Gamble is one of the world's largest consumer goods companies with annual sales in excess of $40 billion. In the 1990s it lurched through a series of crises, which destroyed internal morale, led to a slump in sales and profits and resulted in a collapse in the share price. In June 2000 a long-term P&G insider, Alan 'A.G.' Lafley, was appointed as CEO and undertook a simple but deep-rooted change programme. He commented: 'I had to come up with something quickly to get people focused. I didn't want everyone sitting around worrying that our stock price had dropped in half.' [13]

His solution was to focus back onto the ten best selling brands: 'It's a basic strategy that worked for me in the Navy. I learned there that even when you've a complex business, there's a core and that core is what generates most of the cash.' [14]

In just two years Lafley had turned P&G around. Annual cost savings of some $2 billion were delivered and the share price went up by 70 per cent at a time when world stock markets were falling. The success was built on radical change by focusing on just a few key areas.

TALKING TELEPHONE NUMBERS

It is not just a matter of selling change to a company's own employees. Sometimes outsiders – customers and suppliers – must be convinced of specific benefits as well.

A few years ago the UK telephone industry had to introduce extra digits into many telephone numbers simply to accommodate the exploding demand for mobiles, faxes, internet access and so on. They spent millions on telling consumers, in huge detail, what would happen, but the change was unpopular and at times chaotic.

BT had forgotten that the single most important thing was to tell customers (and their own staff who had to respond to the criticism) that users would benefit substantially from more telephone lines and the ability to use more devices. This would more than compensate for a little temporary disruption. Customers were told all about the *process* – which was painful – but not the *benefits* to them – which were desirable.

Take symbolic actions

Change programmes need widespread support inside and outside the business. One of the best ways to engender that is to do highly visible things that illustrate change is underway. I have three personal experiences of this.

SELL THE ROLLS

When I become CEO of an old-fashioned UK company some years ago my employment package included a chauffeur-driven blue Rolls-Royce and a vast office. The company's share price had barely moved in the past ten years and there was a huge amount to be done. The company needed root and branch change which would take three years, but within the first month I sold the car and replaced it with a more functional BMW and revamped my office to create two new ones.

Now the truth is, my gestures were expensive. The (rather old) Rolls was worth less than a new BMW. The new offices were pricey. But I know that people inside and outside the company noticed and it reinforced the idea of ' we are doing things differently from now on'.

THAT RICE PUDDING AGAIN

I mentioned in Chapter 8 that one of my early McKinsey consulting projects was for a major UK bank which needed to radically reduce its bureaucracy and costs. It discovered and did away with the redundant daily rice pudding in the chairman's dining room.

The internal change team project leader was delighted to have uncovered this symbol of the *ancien régime* and in internal communications it became a key anecdote of how things were being modernised. The bank went on to reduce staff and headcount dramatically and became one of the best managed banks in the world.

THE NEW LOBBY LEADS TO A NEW FIRM

I worked with the senior partner of a large accounting firm who was in the process of leading a major change programme following a merger. This required a new remuneration structure, changed policies on recruitment, a corporate name change, a new logo, different business unit leaders and a major reorganisation.

One of the most visible acts – to both staff and clients – was to totally re-design the entrance lobby (at some considerable cost). Initially this produced hoots of derision from some of the senior partners, but to more junior staff and clients it signalled real change in progress.

As it happened, the people who were exerting the most negative influence on the overall change programme were also those who were most vocal in their criticism of the new lobby. Quite quickly the others sidelined them as being simply 'anti-change'. And that paved the way for many of the more fundamental reforms that were required.

Set up early wins

The success of change programmes is proven by actual results judged by hard numbers:

- Reduced costs
- Improved sales
- Contracts won

Success in a change programme is not a matter of producing newsletters or having meetings. It's a matter of visible improvement in areas accepted as important. If tangible success can be identified and communicated early on, it will give people more confidence in the whole process. Some of these early victories can be and should be 'manufactured'.

- 'We said we would reduce debtor days from 60 to 50 and we have.'
- 'We said we had to cut out our ten least profitable lines. We have identified them and they have now gone.'
- 'We said we would improve customer satisfaction and the survey shows it has gone up by 10 per cent.'

When planning change, the CEO should work out some targets which can be unambiguously achieved early on. Soft targets they may well be but none-the-less satisfying in giving people a sense of achievement.

Communicate

Change produces uncertainty and people need information to reassure them. 'Into an information vacuum flows rubbish, mistruths and falsehoods.' During a change programme the project leaders need to put a disproportionate amount of effort into explaining what is happening and why. Suppliers and customers need to understand the implications of change processes for their business relationships whilst employees must be sold on the ideas of the benefits not just to the company but to themselves as individuals.

All forms of communication should be used to support change but the message must be kept simple and unpretentious and repeated often. Employee meetings, mass e-mailing, newsletters, posters, sometimes even TV and press advertising can be used. Those advertisements that appear in business magazines and newspapers when a company changes its name are as much for the benefit of the employees as they are for the other readers.

Public and investor relations become important as *internal* communications devices. In times of change, employees will see comments about their business from respected third parties such as journalists, analysts and shareholders as carrying considerable weight. Positive comment is a strong endorsement of the programme. Those wanting to derail the process will use external criticism to aid their cause.

One powerful philosophical idea is that if there is no word for a concept, such as 'freedom', then the concept might as well not exist. A change programme needs to have a language and concepts of its own which help to describe what is happening. Change usually means going from one place to another. It is important to try to describe the starting point and the destination using metaphors and analogies that the people can understand.

Change programmes often have a theme. GE described their change programme as 'Work-Out'. It was along the idea of working smarter, not harder, and identifying and stopping unnecessary tasks.

Jack Welch explained: '*Work-Out* meant just what the words implied; taking unnecessary work out of the system.'[15]

When Lou Gerstner wanted to make IBM more client focused, he created a programme called 'Bear Hug' which required senior managers to visit at least five major customers and write a report. He observed: '*Bear Hug* became the first step in IBM's cultural change. It was an important way to emphasize that the customer was going to drive everything we did.'[16]

When the accounting firm KPMG wanted to focus its professionals on a new name following a merger, they called the programme 'KPMG Means Business'. It became a consistent slogan used in all communications.

CANON LOOKED BACKWARDS FOR A CHANGE MODEL

It is a powerful communications device to root an initiative in history. In their book *Maximum Leadership 2000* Charles Farkas and his colleagues described the huge change programme at the Japanese electronics and equipment firm Canon.

The chairman Ryuzaburo Kaku decided to decentralise what had been a very rigid business and devolve power to make it more flexible and commercially successful. To capture people's imagination he described the change in terms of a period of Japanese history.

The 'new' Canon would best succeed if it was managed as Japan was 'managed' during the Tokugawa era of samurai rule, the period from 1603 to 1867 during which wealthy Japanese noblemen divided the country into domains and ruled the nation as a collection of prosperous fiefdoms, sometimes warring, but often coexisting because of pacts with mutual benefits. 'Studying the period,' Kaku says, 'made me think one could do it that way now, too, because of the beauty of the balance of centralised power and decentralised control.'[17]

A strong 'story' makes it much easier to explain the change being undertaken.

Summary

- Organisational change is very difficult to achieve because of the inherently conservative nature of human beings.
- Change is easier to implement when a company is felt to be in a crisis.
- A transition team with resources needs to be created to manage major change projects.
- Change programmes focused on a few key benefits have the best chance of success.
- Symbolic acts demonstrate that radical change is underway.
- Early victories based on meeting specific goals give momentum to a change programme.
- CEOs and change leaders must communicate, perhaps over-communicate, at every step of the way, as lack of information is the main barrier to accepting change.

10 Picking winners: investment

*A successful enterprise must be good at investing the cash that
it earns from operations or raises from banks and shareholders.
It must get a better return on this cash than it pays for the use
of the money. CEOs control the process of capital allocation by
building a team to assess projects to select those with the best
return relative to risk.*

This chapter is about what to do with cash. It is about how a company finds investments that will yield superior returns. Chapter 8 on operations was about how to generate cash from a business. This one is about how to put cash back into it.

Capital – as in cash to be invested – behaves in the opposite way to water. It always flows to the high ground. It finds its way to the projects or investments with the highest return. Or should do. The whole stock market and banking systems are designed to make this happen. To send capital to the companies that make best use of it. And the most effective companies are those that consistently pick the best projects and acquisitions.

The allocation of capital is a black art of extraordinary complexity if you go by the thousands of textbooks and armies of corporate finance professors and investment banking analysts. In theory, of course, it is very simple. It is the process of assessing risk and reward.

This book is written from the perspective of the CEO. The person whose job it is to shape and lead the business. CEOs must make decisions about how to invest cash. These are not day-to-day management issues but moments of discontinuity when projects or deals are brought to the CEO for assessment. They must have mechanisms in place to select the best returns.

Do you invest $1 million in an additional small manufacturing plant in an old steel town just outside Cleveland which will almost certainly generate $200,000 a year in cash, or do you commit that $1 million to open and staff up a new office in Rio de Janeiro which may produce $5 million of new sales in a new market? The answer is probably Cleveland, but Rio is so much nicer in the winter.

A company has many competing calls on its cash. These include new equipment, new projects, acquisitions, buying back its own shares or paying dividends to shareholders. The cash should go to the area which benefits shareholders most. This is normally funding investments with a high return and low risk. If you can find them.

Assessing the value of a proposal

Any investment project or acquisition is intended to produce a stream of cash flows into the business. Trying to pick the winners really boils down to two questions:

- How much will those cash flows actually be?
- What are these future cash flows worth today?

The first question is all about making the right assumptions and taking steps to reduce the risk of those assumptions being wrong. This is the main issue and is covered later in this chapter. The second question is the subject of much hot debate and can lead to managers becoming so bound up in the mathematics and mechanics of the investment process that they lose sight of the likely success or failure of the project itself.

What is the present value of future cash?

Imagine being presented with two envelopes and told to choose one only. The first contains a crisp $100 bill and the second a paper guaranteeing to hand over $100 in twelve months' time. You would obviously prefer the one with the cash as it has value now. You can spend it. There is no risk.

If by chance you ended up with the second envelope – the promise of $100 in a year's time – you could go to a bank and ask them how much cash they would give you today to 'buy' your piece of paper. Assuming there was no risk of the money not being delivered in a year, the amount the bank will pay you today is directly linked to prevailing interest rates. If interest rates are 10 per cent a year then the bank will probably give you about $90 for your paper. The logic being that $90 invested today at 10 per cent interest will produce about $100 in a year's time. In other words the *discounted present value* of a certain $100 a year away is about $90 at a 10 per cent *discount rate*.

To you, the cost of obtaining the $90 today is an annual payment of 10 per cent. Your *cost of capital* is 10 per cent.

For a company, the question of what future cash is worth today comes down to two issues:

- How much does it cost us to get cash from banks and shareholders (i.e. what is the company's *cost of capital*)?
- What is the *risk* that the promised money will not materialise?

Cost of capital

A company must know what it really costs it to obtain money as that tells managers how good projects have to be to create value. Projects have to earn more than the cost of capital or they are 'pouring money down the drain'.

The company's cost of capital is a mixture of its cost of debt (essentially interest charges) and cost of equity (shareholders' expectations of dividend payments and share price rises). The mixture of the two is commonly called the weighted average cost of capital or WACC.

There are volumes of theory on this, but most companies have a

WACC of between 7 and 10 per cent. It depends on the volatility of their earnings and the amount of debt they have. If your cost of capital is high because, for example, your company has a poor credit rating, then you must try to solve this problem as it will give an advantage to competitors who may be able to undertake projects which you find impossible to justify. One of the main advantages of corporate size is that big, well-managed businesses normally have access to capital on far better terms than small operators.

In theory you can use the company's own cost of capital as the discount rate to evaluate the value today of future cash flows, assuming those future flows are certain. But, in fact, they are not certain and the second element is the risk that those cash flows will not come through as planned.

The risk premium

The *cost of capital* is what it actually costs the company to obtain cash. The *hurdle rate* is what some companies feel they must obtain from an investment to justify taking the risk.

All good projects must produce returns greater than the cost of capital. But some projects will fail. The theory recognises this by saying a proposed project must return not just the cost of capital but a premium over this to reflect risk. It's a good theory, but it seems to place a lot of effort on trying to calculate what the risk premium might be, rather than focusing on actions to mitigate or reduce that risk.

I believe that trying to adjust for risk by changing the discount rate used for each project is simply wrong because of the managerial behaviour it causes. The cost of capital is a fact. The risk inherent in a project is conjecture.

People get very excited about what hurdle rate to use in valuing future cash flows and try to use bigger rates to reflect greater uncertainty about the future. Spending too much time worrying about this can be counter-productive. The real issue is predicting the future cash flows and taking steps to reduce the risk of the assumptions being wrong.

This prediction is both the art and the science of running an enterprise. Debating the discount rate at length is more akin to trying to read tea-leaves or seeking the future in the entrails of a dead goat. It is focusing on the wrong issue.

The 'right' discount rate

The real issue for company executives and the CEO is choosing *among* various investment projects and *alternative* uses of cash. The cost of the cash for investment does not change.

The best way to do this is to always use the same 'cost of money', the same discount rate in all calculations, and then try to analyse projects in such a way that the relative risk is assessed. To illustrate the point, here are two examples:

- A regional newspaper company must have printing presses close to or in the cities served by its newspapers to reduce physical delivery time and cost. Printing presses wear out. Buying a new press does more for the value of the business than simply replacing old equipment. It may provide extra colour pages, quicker printing and extra features like the ability to insert leaflets. A printing press might cost $10 million but the returns from this investment can be very accurately calculated. Because it simply continues and enhances an existing business, it's a very low-risk investment with a predictable outcome.
- A magazine company grows by launching new titles. To launch a title managers have to make an estimate of the potential readership and the likely advertising income. Until the title is on the streets they do not know if people will really buy it. Also they do not know if a rival will launch a near-identical product and thus split the market. A lot of money has to be risked up front on preparation, dummy editions and

marketing so it's a highly risky investment that may be a big hit or miss.

It is quite possible that both the newspaper and the magazine companies have the same cost of capital so there is no logic in using different discount rates for the projects. The challenge is to distinguish between the high risk and low risk and make judgements accordingly.

Payback period

This is one of the most established ways of looking at projects and predates the computer spreadsheet. It's a simple question: How many months or years do we have to wait to get our money back?

As with all methods, it relies on projections of upfront costs and future income. Some people do not even bother to discount back the present value of future cash.

The concept of the payback period is the intuitive method used by many entrepreneurs. It does have the merit of simplicity but is biased against projects which have returns far off in the future and makes projects with quick returns look the most attractive.

Net present value: NPV

Net present value is the value today of a project.

All cash inflows and outflows are put into a computer model. Future flows are recalculated back to give their present value at a discount rate. Projects with NPVs of more than zero are deemed to be value creating.

The problem with NPV is that the apparent value of the project is hugely changed by the discount rate used. A discount rate of 10 per cent will make many projects appear to have positive NPVs. A discount rate of 20 per cent might make all of those projects look nonviable. The NPV can also be greatly affected by assumptions about what will happen many years into the future.

If all projects have the same risk and the same discount rate can be used for each one, NPV is a useful mathematical tool. But in fact the world does not work this way. Projects differ.

Internal rate of return: IRR

IRR is a simple concept and a complex calculation. It is a statement of the value of a project expressed as the annual return achieved on the cash invested.

The logic is that a project requires cash to go into it at the beginning in the expectation of cash coming out of it at the end. On balance, what do the cash flows coming back represent in terms of 'interest' being earned on the cash flows going in?

The higher the IRR, the 'better' the project is. An IRR of 10 per cent implies that we get back 10 cents a year, every year, on each and every dollar invested. An IRR of 15 per cent suggests 15 cents a year.

An IRR calculation does not require an estimate of a discount rate. It simply compares the value of projected streams of cash to the cash put in. The problem with IRR is that, again, it does not distinguish between risky and safe projects. Thus the IRR of the newspaper press purchase and the magazine launch in the above example may be identical, but the risks are vastly different.

Lots of analysis but little insight

All the above approaches rest on the assumption that the cash flow predictions are correct. If the predictions are wrong, no amount of modelling will make the assessment of the project valid.

The huge danger with NPV or IRR is that managers actually start to believe they mean something. They mean nothing if the projected cash flow is wrong. I have sat in too many meetings where managers promoting a project get all excited because 'The IRR is over 20 per cent.' All that means is that the wholly theoretical future cash flows, when compared mathematically to the all-too-real proposed cash to be invested, spit out a certain number from their spreadsheet.

IRRs and NPVs are easily manipulated. Inward cash flows close to the start of a project seem to be worth more than those near the end because of the effect of present value. Commitments in a contract to invest huge sums in ten years' time (all too real when the time arrives) look quite small in IRR and NPV terms.

THE DANGER OF MODELS

I remember the first time I used a Lotus 123 spreadsheet on a computer. It was a simple and clever program. At the time I got my hands on it in 1984 I thought I had discovered the Philosopher's Stone.

Lotus and its successors and competitors produced one of the most powerful and yet dangerous tools of modern business. The spreadsheet. It is a wonderful way of modelling the likely operation of a business in the future. But it also creates the dangerous delusion that every newly minted MBA graduate has forecasting powers superior to those of Nostradamus and the Delphic Oracle.

The computer industry has long recognised the acronym GIGO: Garbage In, Garbage Out. All CEOs contemplating major investment projects and acquisitions should have this prominently displayed on their wall. The danger with the spreadsheet and its ability, at the touch of a key, to change assumptions and predictions is that people spend less time thinking about the likely outcome of events and more time running scenarios. The belief is that those different scenarios actually do represent alternative outcomes rather than just mathematical curiosities.

Lotus, by the way, got crushed by what had been a small competitor called Microsoft and ended up absorbed into IBM. Bet that outcome didn't appear in their spreadsheet models back in 1984.

THE NEW WAY AT IBM

Before Lou Gerstner took over IBM in April 1993 the company was famous for its long-winded project appraisal process which was based on executives making lengthy and complex presentations using carefully and expensively produced overhead projector slides or 'foils'.

Gerstner felt that the performance in the presentation obscured the true value of the project and he demanded a new approach.

> Gerstner instead asked for written proposals in advance then spent the meeting interrogating his executives. On at least one occasion he walked into a conference room and ripped out the projector's power cord. And he kept documents. If you said that an investment of $20 million would generate $60 million in new revenue you would be back in his office a year later if the revenues did not materialise.[1]

Best case – worst case

The simplest and perhaps best way of forcing people to think about investment risks is to model best- and worst-case scenarios using optimistic and pessimistic assumptions. Looking at a project on the basis that sales will only achieve 80 per cent of the targets gives a real insight into how bad it might be if things went wrong.

Getting a feel for the payback period or NPV or IRR for competing investments under best-case and worst-case assumptions will often help in making the right choice. But of course it all comes back to making good predictions of what will really happen.

Making the correct assumptions

All investment analysis is based on assumptions. How do you reduce the risk of error in the estimates? How do you try to ensure that the projections come true? It starts with trying to understand the market. All businesses operate within a market that sometimes grows and sometimes shrinks.

Is the market infinite?

As you read this, a strategic planner in one of the world's brew-eries will be forecasting the market for beer consumption next year. Others, in competing companies, will be doing the same.

Almost certainly, if you add up all the predicted growth from all of these plans, you will come to a number far bigger than the total growth predicted for the entire industry. Companies are inherently bullish about their own future.

Optimism is a wonderful trait. We all want out businesses, our products and brands to be successful. Most companies assume they will gain market share. The danger is that when these assumptions go into a model, they will predict revenues far in excess of what will actually be produced in most cases.

THE TRIUMPH OF HOPE OVER EXPERIENCE

I used to work in an advertising agency which, like all advertising agen-cies, was very keen to stress how big it was by publishing its 'billings' – the amount of money it handles each year on behalf of clients. Trade magazines like *Campaign* in the UK and *Advertising Age* in the USA would publish league tables of agencies based on their annual billings. The bigger the number, the higher up the table and the happier the own-ers and managers of the agency were.

My job was to produce our annual league table number but I quickly re-alised that our claimed billings were much higher than our real activity. When I asked why, I was given methodology explanations of mind-numbing complexity.

As a matter of curiosity I asked a friend at *Campaign* to add up the claimed billings of the top 100 agencies. The answer produced a num-ber which was 30 per cent bigger than the entire advertising industry. I asked my friend if this worried *Campaign*. 'Not much,' he said. All agencies exaggerated by about the same amount so the relative rankings were probably accurate. And anyway who cares?

So, is exaggeration a victimless crime? Not when people use the claimed numbers in business plans to justify investments.

The questions to ask

When looking at a proposal for an acquisition or a new project there are basic questions to ask.

- Do the sales projections require an increase in market share? If so, is the business actually growing faster than the market? Why is this and can this be sustained?
- Does the margin grow over time? If so, why? Are we planning to put our prices up to boost margins? If so, why will competitors and consumers let us get away with it?
- Are the costs staying flat or going down? How can this be done? Is it improved productivity or a new technology? Will the work force and suppliers accept this?

The truth is that most businesses grow at about the same pace as their market; margins stay about the same because costs rise in line with inflation. Of course there are exceptions, but any business plan that is based on an exception needs very careful scrutiny.

Levels of risk

Wager a dollar on an untried horse with a price of 25 to 1 and you are taking a big risk. But the bookmaker will give you a big reward. Back the favourite, which has won twice over the same course and distance, at 2 to 1, and your risk is much less, but so will the winnings be.

In a business project or acquisition the risk becomes greater as the outcome becomes more uncertain. The risk of a project is nothing to do with its size or the price you pay. It is about the likelihood that your predictions of future cash flows will be wrong.

Figure 10.1 **Investment risks**

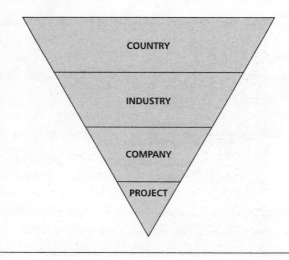

Valuing the projected cash flows is very simple mathematics. The issue is, have you put the right numbers into the spreadsheet? Normally the amount of cash required upfront can be assessed reasonably well as it is based on containable costs. It is predicting the future that is difficult and this comes down to assessing the risk that the predictions will not come true.

At the most macro level capital seeks out countries or economies which look attractive and safe. Typically these include the USA and western Europe. Capital shuns those which look risky. For example Romania, Africa and Indonesia. No matter how high the projected return on a particular project, if there is a risk of losing your investment altogether for political or currency reasons, the project will not be attractive. It is about *country* risk.

Within a national market capital seeks out industries with high, or perceived high, growth which should lead to high return. Technology and healthcare are seen as high growth. Steel manufacture and clothing are low growth. It is about *industry* risk and expected growth rates.

Figure 10.2 **Risk inherent in a project**

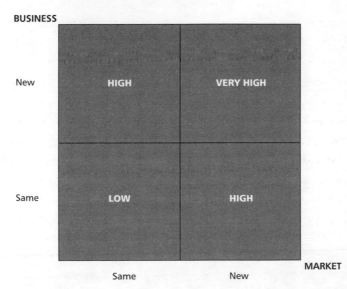

Within an industry capital will flow to those firms that seem to have a good story and good managers. This is evidenced by high share price to earnings multiples and safe credit ratings. It is about *company* risk and reputation.

Within their own company managers must be good at selecting the best projects, acquisitions and investment. They must have ways of picking winners and judging *project* risk. Companies that prove to be good users of capital will get a good reputation and will find capital easier to obtain in the future. Success breeds success.

The risks inherent in a deal increase as the acquirer moves away from their own business and their own market (Figure 10.2). Companies who buy their competitors in their home market take the least risk and are able to do the most effective due diligence. Those who move into new geographic markets by buying the local equivalent of themselves, or venture into new business in their home market, take higher risks but at least have some knowledge base, either of the industry or the market. Companies who try to acquire businesses in industries they do not know in territories that are new to them, need to have a huge rate of return to justify the risk they are taking.

Reducing risk

Projects and acquisitions fail in financial terms because they do not pay back enough to justify the price. The risk is the risk of things going wrong. The four ways of reducing risk are:

1 Doing due diligence to ensure you really get what you think you are buying.
2 Having a 'champion' who is dedicated to making the project or acquisition work.
3 Making the price paid linked to future performance. The earn-out.
4 Managing the post-deal process well. Integration.

The management of the post-deal process is the subject of the next chapter. The first three issues are covered below.

Due diligence
Due diligence is a much-used phrase in most M&A work. It is just as relevant for a project as it is for an acquisition. What does it really mean?

Due diligence SHOULD mean a thorough and detailed analysis of four elements.

1 Are the assets really there and are the contracts valid (legal)?
2 Are the historical profit and loss numbers accurate (financial)?
3 Is the business model viable and sustainable (commercial)?
4 Are the people honest and committed (human)?

Unfortunately, most due diligence is addressed only to the first two issues. And it is often done by hired professionals from outside the company who are not involved in the risk afterwards. The investigation results in a long, detailed and expensive report from an accounting firm that simply looks at the historic numbers of the target company and reassures that 'what you see is what you get'. Another equally lavish report from a law firm will confirm contracts are valid. Neither says if the business is any good.

These reports certainly can save management careers and reduce legal negligence suits if the acquisition goes wrong but they cannot, and are not intended to, tell you if it is a good business or project. It is the commercial and human due diligence that is so necessary to have. And is so often not done.

The level and scope of this 'real' due diligence should increase with the level of risk inherent in the investment. A seasoned manager who really understands the basic economics of the business being considered should lead the investigating team. Someone who can quickly 'see' and 'smell' when things do not seem right with the numbers. Businesses in the same industry will normally have similar margins and similar dynamics. If something looks odd about a company, it is probably because something is wrong.

I am always amazed when corporate acquirers congratulate themselves in press releases that they have purchased a business with abnormally high operating margins. What they have usually purchased is a business that has been dressed up for sale or one that sustains high margins by some strange, and probably temporary, market anomaly. The best businesses to buy are those that have some margin upside.

CEOs need to involve themselves in commercial due diligence as they can take an overview of the whole business. And they must be held accountable for the investment after it is made.

MOTOROLA'S MESS IN TURKEY

The telecoms company Motorola decided to get into the mobile telephone market in Turkey by way of a deal with a local Turkish conglomerate who had been awarded a wireless licence. The deal gave Motorola a
controlling equity stake in the new business, called Telsim, but required
them to make a series of loans to the new business.

In the end Motorola loaned $2 billion and Nokia $700 million. Both
companies have alleged their Turkish partner cheated them and launched
a series of legal actions. *Fortune* reported a US district judge writing:

> Every preliminary indication is that the defendants (the
> Turkish partners) behind a façade of legitimacy, engaged in
> repeated acts of fraud and chicanery and thereby
> perpetrated and continued to perpetrate, a rather massive
> swindle.[2]

Motorola's motivation for the deal was simply the size and growth
potential of the Turkish market but *Fortune* commented:

> How Motorola and Nokia ended up giving $2.7 billion to
> [Telsim] is a story that anyone who has kissed a stranger in a
> bar after having too much to drink will understand ... Mo-
> torola said they did 'considerable due diligence' but did not
> get Telsim's audited accounts. A Motorola spokesman said,
> 'We asked if we could send in auditors. We asked if we
> could talk to the company's auditors but they [the partners]
> refused' ... Maybe there should be an entry in the [Mo-
> torola] accounts: tuition for lessons learned.[3]

BUYING TROUBLE

I was once involved in the acquisition of a media buying company in France. Typically media buying companies enjoy a gross margin of about 5 per cent: their income is about 5 per cent of their turnover. This reflects the fact they are doing the media-buying task for an advertiser and getting a small commission or fee.

Our target had an income of more like 25 per cent of turnover and a profit margin of some 5 per cent of turnover. This was some five times greater than one of their more 'normal' competitors overseas. The reason was that, far from just buying media time and space, they actually traded in it – acted like a wholesaler by buying it and selling it on. The high margin was their reward for taking a risk.

Due diligence discovered this business model but failed to point out that the French government were planning to make this practice illegal. It was perfectly legal at the time of the deal. This threat this did not appear in the accountants' historical reports but would have emerged from a quiet drink with anyone senior in the advertising industry.

In time a new law was passed and the margins of the business collapsed to more normal levels. This business remained intact but the acquisition price became ludicrous.

Another fact that would have come out of a few informal chats was that one of the shareholders selling the business had recently won the World Poker Championships. Not a disclosure requirement in and of itself, but it is now a question I ask in all proposed transactions!

A project champion

The risk in any investment is that the promised results do not materialise. One of the best ways to guard against this is to have the project championed by the person who made the proposal in the first place and who then sees it through. This project champion will feel passionate about the investment and can be monitored on performance.

The worst investments are those which are introduced to a company by an external broker and which get done for financial reasons by a team of bankers but which do not have a real internal champion to see them through. When analysed after the event, the best investments always seem to be those where you can put someone's name to them.

Earn-outs

This is an automatic way of reducing risk as it, theoretically, links the final price paid for a business or project to the performance of that business or project. It is particularly popular as an acquisition structure in professional service firms and is always some variant on the theme: 'We will buy 51 per cent of your shares now and the remaining 49 per cent at an agreed multiple of future profits in five years' time. The bigger your profits, the more you get.'

It is a very good idea, in theory, as the selling shareholders (who presumably understand their business) have to stay in the company and work to get paid full value. If the business collapses, their remaining 49 per cent becomes worth much less. If the business thrives, they can often make far more on the 49 per cent than they did on the 51.

By and large, the earn-out is a good idea, working in a similar way to the venture capitalists' 'ratchet' which rewards entrepreneurs for high levels of performance. The main problem with earn-outs is the open invitation to manipulation of profit numbers by the selling managers.

The fine details of what can be done to boost profits during an earn-out would provide a thick book in themselves but let me give an example.

PUMPING THE PROFITS

I was involved in assessing a specialist communications firm that had been acquired some years before by a media holding company on an earn-out under which the selling shareholders would be paid six times the profit before tax of the business in the fifth year after the earn-out.

It was intended that the business would form the core of a new division to be built by acquisition. It was now year four and I was asked to join the management team to see how things were doing to prepare for the next stage. Here's what I found out:

- No one from the acquiring holding company had been involved in annual budgeting or monthly reporting for three years. The business had been left to run itself.
- The budget for the next twelve months – the earn-out year – projected a huge profit.
- Most senior staff had been told they were subject to a two-year pay freeze but 'it would all be made up to them very soon'.
- Virtually every discretionary cost in the business had been cut. No office cleaning was being done – staff took out their own trash each night. Window cleaning contracts had been cancelled. What once had been free coffee, soft drinks and snacks, had been stopped. Staff brought their own.
- The three most senior managers (all shareholders) had hardly claimed any expenses and were, in a way, subsidising business costs from their own pockets. Remember they would be paid $6 for each $1 of profit, so each time they saved a $1 of cost it was worth $6 to them.
- Debtor days, the measure of how quickly invoices were being paid, had risen from 25 days to 65 days. The reason was that early payment discount incentives had been cancelled to increase declared profits.

All this was duly reported back to the corporate centre, which decided that far from creating a new division they would sell this business. A massive earn-out payment was made to the vendors – who had done nothing illegal or improper but simply, sensibly, managed the business for their own short-term profit. The company was sold to new owners a few months later.

The lesson of earn-out problems (like those described above) is to put in a senior manager on day one. Preferably a new finance director who is clear that his or her allegiance is to the corporate purchasers rather than the earn-out managers. Also, all sale and purchase agreements need to require that there be no material changes to business practice during the earn-out period.

Having reported the horror story, however, I should say that the earn-out (when properly managed) remains one of the safest and most effective ways of making acquisitions as it keeps founding managers involved and incentivised.

Summary

- Companies have to select projects which deliver the best return on capital. In choosing among projects the real issue is assessing their relative risk. The riskier the project, the higher the return required.
- Too much emphasis on the mathematics of calculations, NPVs and IRRs can distract from the real issues of accurately predicting cash flows.
- Risk can be reduced by careful due diligence and by having price adjustment formulae built into the deal.
- The best way to make an investment successful is to have a project champion and to monitor promised performance.

11   Managing transactions: deals

Mergers and acquisitions help companies grow. They are used to build a strategic position in a market and can yield substantial cost-savings from consolidation. However, the majority of such deals do not create value for shareholders. The processes of doing a deal and of integration afterwards are tasks that the CEO must lead personally.

Businesses have to grow to satisfy their shareholders, managers and employees and sometimes their customers as well. But growth cannot normally be achieved only from organic sources. Simply selling more and gradually expanding will not be enough. Most companies must buy or merge with others at some time. Mergers and Acquisitions – M&A – are a required skill for CEOs.

The last chapter was about making investment decisions. The purchase of, or merger with, another business is one of the biggest of these investment decisions. This chapter is about how to make these deals work.

Management consultants love to cite statistics to show that most mergers and acquisitions destroy shareholder value. This is not surprising as they put themselves front and centre to help in post-merger integration. McKinsey & Co reported that 'up to 80 per cent of M&A deals completed in the 1990s failed to justify the equity that funded them'.[1] In another study the same firm showed that 40 per cent of mergers failed to capture the identified cost-savings.[2]

Another consulting firm, Deloitte & Touche, found that a failed merger or acquisition was the leading cause of problems for 57 per cent of large UK businesses that had to call in their reorganisation practice.[3] Professor Robert Bruner of the Darden School of Business looked at mergers and acquisitions over a thirty-year period and concluded only '37 per cent created value for buyers'.[4] The *Financial Times* reported research that '60 to 70 per cent of all mergers fail'.[5]

Philip Watts, chairman of Royal Dutch/Shell, comments: 'Most acquisitions destroy value for the shareholder. People either pay too much, or they don't implement the acquisition properly.'[6]

Investment bankers, on the other hand, will tell you that M&A are a vital and irreplaceable part of building a growing company. Corporate lawyers will happily support this view. Not surprising when professional fees can be 2 per cent of the value of a deal. Even in huge transactions like the $150 billion AOL Time Warner merger, where the percentage is lower, the fees alone were estimated at $120 million,[7] a bumper payday for the professionals and a built-in incentive for them to want deals to happen.

In the boom year of 2000 the total value of some 40,000 M&A deals around the world was nearly $3,500 billion.[8] The fees on that would have been around a staggering $50 billion, which funded a lot of summer homes in the Hamptons and Hampshire.

But there are examples of M&A that worked. The oil giant BP was created by a series of deals including Amoco and Arco. The merger of Glaxo and SmithKline has been hailed as a success. The combination of Royal Bank of Scotland and NatWest has produced huge savings. Unilever and Procter & Gamble have completed many value-creating purchases.

The *Wall Street Journal* reported that in his twenty-year reign as chief executive of General Electric Jack Welch completed 993 acquisitions with a total value of $130 billion and sold 408 businesses for a total of $10.6 billion.[9] When Welch retired in 2001 the share price of GE was 5,000 per cent higher than on the day he took over and its annual earnings of $12.5 billion were eight times greater than when he started. It would have been impossible to create GE (or most of the world's other great companies) without acquisitions and mergers.

So, does M&A, on balance, create or destroy value? In truth the evidence is somewhat contradictory. What is without doubt true is that most great businesses have been built using M&A as a tool and successful CEOs must learn to be good at it. Doing deals and, even more important, integrating the businesses afterwards cannot be easily delegated. The CEO needs to lead the process.

Why deals fail

There are three main reasons why deals fail to create value:

- The deal is based on a flawed concept of how an industry would evolve and the expected new business model fails to materialise. Examples include AOL with Time Warner and Vivendi with almost everything.
- The buyer pays too much – more than can ever be realised in synergies or savings – because of over-enthusiastic bidding.
- The promised, and correctly valued, synergies and savings are not delivered. This is the most common cause of value destruction.

Deals designed to 'break the mould' usually do not. It is hard to imagine how a deal could create a 'new paradigm' (as the dot.com bankers liked to claim). The M&A tool should only be used to make what is there better rather than to create something revolutionary. Dell, Intel and Microsoft owe most of their success to innovation and organic growth. Deals are the icing on the cake, which helped businesses like Microsoft to achieve scale but did not fundamentally change the company.

Creating conglomerates out of weak businesses simply because they could be acquired cheaply does not create value. Putting together two bad companies does not make one good one – no matter how cheap the price.

Overpayment, for a logical deal, is a different problem. It is often a function of timing by buying at the top of a business cycle, the easy availability of credit and investment funds and the danger of getting involved in a competitive auction. The lesson is probably not to be a buyer when there is a lot of cash chasing only a few deals and when stock market ratings are at historic highs. At these times it is almost impossible to make a deal work at the price you have to pay.

The real challenge is why 'normal' run-of-the-mill, strategically logical and reasonably priced deals fail. This occurs as a result of poor implementation rather than strategic dreaming or overpayment. Capturing the promises made in a deal is what marks out good CEOs from bad ones. Writing in the *Financial Times* Angus Knowles-Cutler of Deloitte & Touch commented:

> Most often difficulties arose from the failure to
> integrate the acquired business. Integration, or the lack
> of it, is the interlocking thread behind M&A failures.
> Any chief executive about to embark on an acquisition
> needs to ask whether his or her business has the
> appetite and the capability successfully to integrate
> what it has bought. As the champagne corks pop at the
> close of a deal there is a tendency for senior
> management to believe that the immediate hard work is
> over.[10]

The core problem is that for the vast majority of companies implementing deals is not what they normally do well. Post-acquisition or merger integration is a rare corporate event requiring special skills. There are armies of bankers ready to help with the deal process but few experienced managers who know how to make the deal work afterwards.

Hooked on deals

Business commentators will sometimes describe a CEO as a 'deal junkie' – someone who is 'hooked' on the excitement and drama of deal making. It is not a complimentary description.

In fact, the analogy with drug dependency goes beyond just providing some entertainment for headline writers. The stock market can become obsessed by achieving growth in annual earnings. Certainly in the 1990s it was the main measure of success. A CEO who could not deliver earnings growth was in trouble and deals could be made to appear to deliver that growth even when a business was doing poorly. For CEOs who cannot find new profits within their business, deals can be a lifeline.

All too often a merger or acquisition is seen as a way out of trouble rather than as part of an overall strategic plan. The correct managerial solution might be organic growth – but it takes time. The short-term financial engineering solution, the deal, can deliver instant results.

Deals can appear to be earnings-enhancing in the short term, particularly if the acquiring company can use its own highly rated shares to buy another company's more modestly rated profits. The logic is painfully simple. If your company is valued by the stock market at twenty times last year's earnings and you buy another business at the equivalent price of ten times last year's earnings, you have an immediate short-term leap in your own reported earnings per share. As long as the stock market keeps rating your company highly you can keep on doing it.

Writing in the *Financial Times*, columnist John Plender noted that the incentives for managers and CEOs were often to do an aggressive transaction to boost earnings even if it resulted in a long-term weakening of the company's real value. He commented:

> The vested interests at the top of the City food chain in
> favour of frenetic takeovers are very powerful.

Meantime the capital market incentives ensure that
managers are anxious to keep the City in fees. Who can
blame managers, heavily laden with stock options, from
heeding the siren call of the investment bankers who
propose a 'transforming' takeover? Even if it wrecks
the balance sheet the manager still receives a reward for
failure.[11]

COKE'S COLLAPSE

In 2001 *Fortune* commented on the Coca-Cola Company:

The once powerful stock is now trading at $47, right
where it was five years ago. Sales growth of Coke-branded
products has slowed dramatically. Three straight years of
earnings decline have sapped the company's strength
…Coke's fundamental problem is that Doug Ivestor (the
previous CEO) was fixated on deal making and financial
engineering at the expense of marketing and new
products.[12]

Coke did very, very well for a very long time selling sugared water for
a lot more than it cost to bottle it. It created a wonderful worldwide
brand franchise and a superb marketing machine. Coke, if *Fortune* is
right, succumbed to the lure of earnings-enhancing deals and took its eye
off the ball of running the business well.

FAILURE AT FORD

The Ford Motor Company suffered a spectacular collapse under the leadership of chief executive Jacques Nasser. Its market value fell from $50 bil-
lion in March 2001 to $30 billion in March 2002. Annual profits went

from $7.2 billion in 1999 to a loss of $5.5 billion in 2001. Nasser was ousted and replaced by Bill Ford, the great-grandson of the founder Henry Ford.

Forbes commented:

> Nasser's grand plan was to change Ford from a mere car
> manufacturer to a consumer brand company. Nasser
> hatched a scheme to get into Internet activities, car
> retailing, repair shops, even junkyards. They all backfired
> and, worse, they distracted executives from the business of
> designing, building and selling vehicles.[13]

Business Week observed:

> Under Nasser, Ford had fallen into a sorry state of disrepair.
> Its profits, market share, quality and morale were spiralling
> downwards as he tried to turn it into something, anything,
> other than a traditional car company. He acquired Volvo
> Car and Land Rover. The company's $15 billion cash hoard
> dwindled to less than $1 billion.[14]

It seems that deal making had become more important than car making.

THE ALLURE OF BROOKS BROTHERS

Bad deals often arise from developing an irrational emotional attachment to the target company and from the lack of follow-through after the purchase.

In 1988 the venerable and, then, venerated British department store Marks & Spencer was looking to expand into the USA and decided to do it by way of acquisition. In a hundred years of corporate history this would be their first major deal and they settled on Brooks Brothers, the upmarket and preppy retailer who could lay claim to dressing Wall Street in its signature button-down shirts and who had made (and still owned) the jacket in which Abraham Lincoln was shot. The autocratic chairman and chief executive of M&S Derek Rayner – the first non-family member to be chairman of the group – led the deal.

In her book *The Rise and Fall of Marks & Spencer* Judi Bevan notes that Robert Campeau, who was selling Brooks Brothers to finance ambitious expansion plans in other businesses, appointed the highly aggressive banker Bruce Wasserstein to manage the sale.

> In the event Campeau, backed up by Wasserstein, was able to persuade Rayner to pay $750m for Brooks Brothers, a sum that was about twice what his own executives thought it was worth. But Rayner was the chairman and he was enamoured with Brooks Brothers clothing, which was in large part aimed at men of Rayner's age and taste. Dazzled by the heady climate and Campeau's lavish hospitality, he lost touch with reality. What, he must have asked himself, was a few dollars more if one were buying a trophy brand recognised throughout the world?[15]

Brooks Brothers was, essentially, a stand-alone American business with few managerial or operating synergies with the UK store chain. Assessing the failure, the *Sunday Telegraph* commented:

> M&S also failed abysmally to market its new subsidiary properly. As a result the company's lucrative market place of high quality men's-wear was rapidly captured by other more appealing brands. Finally M&S struggled to absorb the Brooks culture. This included paying large commissions to sales staff, something that was entirely alien to M&S's salaried world.[16]

The M&S management stubbornly held on but Brooks was ultimately sold in 2001 for $225 million. This was a loss of some $525 million, not to mention thirteen years of poor returns. The true cost to shareholders of M&S was close to $1 billion; a spectacular destruction of shareholder value.

Deals can create value

So, if deals are risky and destructive, why do them at all? The reason is that they can be very successful if done well.

Chief executives are looking to grow their business and have to find opportunities to invest money which will have a return greater than their cost of capital. All businesses have the possibility of investing in new products, of opening up new offices and putting in new equipment to increase capacity and improve efficiency. Buying another business or merging with one just accelerates this process of growth. It has the same effect as organic growth – only faster.

A deal done at the right price and implemented well reduces costs and boosts earnings. The questions are 'What is the right price?' and 'How do you deliver on the expectations upon which the deal was founded?'

The main motivations for deals – mergers or acquisitions – are to:

- consolidate a market,
- acquire a supplier or a distributor,
- enter a new market,
- enter a new industry.

As discussed in Chapter 10, the risk of failure increases as you move away from your own core operations.

Buying or merging with a competitor is frequently called a horizontal, tactical or tuck-in acquisition. It is typical of a consolidation strategy. It is the lowest-risk approach and is usually focused on cost cutting.

Going upstream (buying a supplier) or downstream (buying a distributor) is a vertical acquisition. The main risk is that the business acquired will lose its competitive edge by being integrated into a former business partner. The motive is usually to improve overall margins.

Using an acquisition to go into a new market, or even a new industry, is a strategic move and normally carries the highest level of risk.

Consolidation cuts costs

Consolidation is a tried and tested way to make shareholders rich. Buying up competitors normally brings benefits through removing duplicated activities.

A market served by two companies will be far more efficient than the same market served by dozens of small firms. Now if, and it's a big if, the remaining two competitors do not simply erode each other's margins by head-to-head competition, then their shareholders will enjoy better returns than if they owned a group of small, inefficient businesses.

Not unreasonably, government competition authorities are very sensitive to and suspicious of companies acquiring their competitors, but there is certainly no automatic reason that consumers should suffer. Many such deals are motivated by a desire to be more efficient and to save costs rather than to put up prices.

Generally, buying or merging with competitors is the least risky sort of deal as the management will be very familiar with the economics and issues of both businesses and, therefore, able to capture the cost saving identified. Consolidation also works as it enables resources such as IT systems, accounting back offices and production plants to be shared between two operations. It also allows the closure of the head office of one of the businesses, which can bring substantial savings.

CONSOLIDATION SAVINGS ARE REAL IN RADIO

A typical small music radio station needs at least two studios, one 'on-air' for broadcasting and one 'off-air' for preparation. The programme presenters will probably be freelance talent who are hired in for specific shows. The station needs three or four engineers, four or five full-time production staff led by a full-time programme director and a sales team which may be ten or more, depending on the size of the market. A receptionist will answer calls and deal with visitors. An accounts team controls the cash and a general manager runs the whole thing.

A small station like that can make a decent profit.

Now, assume another very similar station in the same city with a similar type of programming but broadcasting to the same geographic area. Put the two together in the same building and you can have three studios instead of four, perhaps five production staff instead of ten, the same sales team and accountants and it is still run by one general manager.

The benefits of consolidating these two operations are real and substantial. If both stations made profits of $1m each before combination, they will probably make $4 million as a combined entity. Broadcast quality is the same or better as more resources are available for programming which may become more varied. Huge value has been created. Everyone wins.

Vertical integration

A supplier of goods or services to a company expects to make a profit. In a similar way, a distributor will expect to make a margin.

Acquisitions of suppliers and distributors can be attractive as the buyer gets to keep their profit margins. But the risk is always that the acquiring company will fail to manage these businesses as well as when they were independent.

Buying a supplier or a distributor theoretically improves the economics of the acquiring business. For example a newspaper publisher might buy a printing firm (upstream integration) or a chain of newsagents (downstream integration). In both cases there should be benefits from absorbing a company that made profits out of providing a service. However, the acquired business may operate less well under the new ownership, as managers will no longer have to compete for a contract in terms of price or service. They may be complacent that their owner will have to use them no matter how badly they perform.

There may also be a problem with third-party contracts. The acquired business may have provided services to companies who will no longer want to do business with it under new ownership. This can happen, for example, with an advertising agency which has been acquired by a major client. Other advertisers who compete with the new owner may well withdraw their business, fearing leaks of confidential information and conflicts of interest.

Reducing risk in this type of deal is focused on developing the right bonus structures for management to ensure service quality is maintained, and on having discussions with key customers in advance to assess their response to change of ownership.

New markets: international acquisitions

As the market for most goods and services becomes increasingly global, more companies seek to develop beyond their home market. Organic growth by setting up new operations can be very time consuming and expensive.

For manufacturing companies making a specialised locally produced product like wine or cheese, going international is a matter of finding distributors and retailers in markets outside their home country. This model does, of course, also work for other industries like software producers – the most famous and obvious example being Microsoft. In effect, they are like the vineyard as they grow and press the intellectual grapes in Redmond, Washington, and simply need worldwide distribution and service.

However, for most businesses gaining access to world markets means making acquisitions, as the route of organically setting up simply takes too long and does not provide scale.

To go into a new geographic market by acquiring a similar business in that market is a moderate risk. The acquirer will understand the business model and may be able to capture some cost synergies across international borders. However, operating in a different culture with a different legal system and perhaps a foreign language presents huge challenges. Success is usually based on having strong local management.

EMAP'S ERRORS

The UK magazine publisher EMAP agreed to buy an American magazine business called Petersen for $1.5 billion in 1998. At first sight it seemed that the US business was similar to their UK operation. But in fact the USA and UK markets operate in fundamentally different ways. In the UK most magazines are sold by newsagents and cover-price income is an important element of revenue. In the USA most magazines are distributed by postal subscription at very low prices simply to obtain a large readership base for the sale of advertising.

EMAP got its assumptions horribly wrong and they were forced to sell the company three years later with a loss of nearly $1 billion. The *Wall Street Journal* described the deal as 'disastrous' and quoted an industry expert as saying, 'they put too many Brits in charge, instead of relying on Americans to run the business'.[17]

It is dangerous to assume that the conditions of the domestic market are replicated elsewhere.

REED'S SUCCESS

Another UK publisher, Reed Elsevier, had the opposite experience when it bought its way into the huge American market with the acquisition of the educational publishing business of Harcourt General Inc. They used the eight-month period it took to obtain regulatory approvals to thoroughly plan integration and select American executives to run the resulting business. They chose to run the business in a very different way from their European operations. The acquisition was very popular with investors and *The Times* described it as 'textbook'. It quoted one of the US managers: 'There hasn't been the clash of cultures you might expect between an American company based in Florida and a British-Dutch parent headquartered in London.'[18]

New industries

The riskiest deal of all is where management use their shareholders' money to go into a new business – one different from their current operations. Shareholders do not normally want management doing this type of transaction because as investors they can do it for themselves by buying the separate businesses.

When the water and sewage company Vivendi decided to go into the USA music and entertainment business, it had a flimsy strategy based on distributing US content through European mobile-phone systems. The reality was that recording music had little to do with reprocessing water and French industrialists did not understand Hollywood. Catastrophe followed.

A successful and cash rich company in an industry which seems threatened may choose to use its strong balance sheet and management skills to diversify in a radical way. This was typical of the tobacco companies who could see litigation and regulation problems coming and branched out into food and services.

Philip Morris acquired Miller Brewing, Kraft General Foods and Nabisco Foods. It is hard to say whether these deals really created value or if shareholders would have been better with special dividends, but the risk of building a conglomerate is certainly reduced by buying established market leaders.

Negotiating 'win–win' solutions

All deals need an element of negotiation. Who gets what? How are the spoils shared? In a merger it is classically what proportion of the resulting company goes to each of the original groups of shareholders.

In an acquisition it will obviously be the purchase price, but also issues of subjective judgement to do with evaluation of outstanding debts, severance terms for senior managers and ongoing contractual obligations of the vendors of the business.

A joint venture is the most complex to negotiate as the interests and behaviour of the parties going forward must be reflected in legal agreements.

There is a huge body of literature on negotiating skills and techniques. Most come back down to the fundamental idea of seeking win–win solutions. That is an outcome which brings benefit to both sides.

The CEO must ultimately lead all major negotiations even if they are only physically required at the very end to sign the agreement. The actual negotiators need to be given, by the CEO at the start, very clear instructions about what is the 'bottom line'. The worst thing for a negotiator is to have these fundamentals changed during the process.

All negotiation is a compromise to find solutions acceptable to both parties. There are several excellent books on this.[19] Here are my suggestions for negotiation:

- Do a lot of listening and ask a lot of questions. The objective is not to tell the other side what you want (at least not to begin with) but simply to find out ALL their issues.
- Look for solutions that please them without giving away anything dear to you. What someone else really wants is surprisingly often not a problem for you and can be easily agreed.
- Take the lead in process management. Offer that you or one of your team of advisers is the one drafting discussion documents,

making lists and organising meetings. Having control of the process will make it far more likely that you get your desired result.

- When the time comes, as late as possible, list all your own requirements and then get all the issues from both sides on the table BEFORE you start agreeing to any individual items. Ask many times 'Are you sure there is nothing else?' before you get down to looking for solutions.
- Try not to agree on an issue-by-issue basis but go for a complete package. Before you move to an agreement on a package, play back what you believe has been agreed to ensure the other side understand the same things that you do. When you are sure you both have the same interpretation then, and only then, say 'I agree'.
- Tell anyone who will listen that negotiating along the lines of 'You want 100. I will give 50. Let's split the difference to 75' is intellectually bankrupt and pointless. And then, towards the end of the discussion, do just that – having established a very high number on your side of the deal. Although it *is* the 'wrong' approach, human beings are hugely drawn to the 'let's split the difference' idea and will find it fair.
- Always check your ego at the door and always be prepared to be shown up, belittled, patronised and humiliated. If you are negotiating with someone who wants to prove they are smarter than you – indulge them; be shown to be their inferior. Simply make sure you get what you want from the deal. They will be so busy scoring points off you, they are likely to give away the shop.
- Ensure there is always some higher authority that you have to get final permission from. 'I like this package and now I must sell it to my board.' The big egos like to point out they are the ultimate decision maker at the table. It puts them at a substantial disadvantage in any negotiating session, as it is hard for them to say anything other than yes or no to a specific proposal. Even if you are the ultimate decision maker, don't admit it.

Making a combination work

Both mergers and acquisitions result in a change of control of the business. Or at least they should do. The key for success is to know from day one who will be in charge and make it unambiguous.

Many mergers and even acquisitions are riddled with political compromise. The concept of joint CEOs is ridiculous. And will always end in tears. Everybody in and associated with a company (staff, customers, suppliers) needs to have a clear idea of who is in charge and what the enlarged company's priorities are. By all means have very strong and autonomous divisional managing directors (many may be called CEOs of a division), but at the top you need just one boss and one policy.

Mergers are different from acquisitions

True mergers are rare. It means a real combining, a mingling of two businesses to create a larger one. It means a mixing of two, often different, cultures. It means synergy in the proper sense that two complementary businesses together are worth more than the two alone.

Accounting rules that allow the sellers of a company to receive shares in the acquirer without paying tax are often called 'mergers' for legal reasons but are really just acquisitions where no cash changes hands. Real mergers need two organisations with complementary needs where the management of both groups *want* the combination to happen and have clear roles in the resulting entity or are happy to leave.

Some mergers are done to give scale. Two regional newspaper companies, for example, may merge to share investment in new, shared printing facilities. Two small banks with complementary branch networks may merge to give better geographic coverage and will make more profit as one bigger bank.

In a true merger the original shareholders end up owning a smaller but more valuable percentage of a larger business.

An acquisition, as the name implies, means a company buys a

business asset. It could simply be an office building or a vehicle. But it is frequently another business. A very large acquisition has many of the characteristics of a merger as the people and the businesses need to be integrated together and even if the shares of the target company have changed hands, the real power in the resulting business is often complex to identify. Small acquisitions are usually much easier to assimilate as they are less likely to change the character and approach of the acquirer.

VIACOM

Viacom, one of the world's largest media companies, was put together in May 2000 through the combination of CBS, the US television and radio business run by Mel Karmazin, and Viacom, the media group including Paramount Studios, MTV and publisher Simon & Schuster, which was constructed by Sumner Redstone.

At the time of the merger (technically a purchase by Viacom) there was speculation that the two, strong-willed entrepreneurs would become co-CEOs. A solution rejected by Karmazin who commented to the *Wall Street Journal*:

> The deal where you take a CEO of one company and
> combine with somebody of another company; these deals
> rarely work. You can't have two people running a company
> day to day. It causes politics; it causes confusion; when it
> comes to making decisions on operations you can't have
> two people doing it.[20]

In the event, Redstone kept the title of CEO and Karmazin was called chief operating officer (COO) but the by-laws of the company were actually changed to make it clear that Karmazin really ran the operations. A legal structure was enacted to ensure that for thirty-six months following the deal Karmazin could not be removed and he was clearly running things day to day. The titles might not be clear but the line of responsibility was unambiguous.

The people dimension
Only in rare cases are mergers and acquisitions simply about assets. In most deals a management team is acquired along with the business. This means where before there was one team, now there are two. This may mean redundancies and will certainly lead to issues of 'turf' and 'who is in charge'.

Writing about John D. Rockefeller (who created Standard Oil through a series of acquisitions) author Daniel Gross comments: 'His greatest contribution, beyond the concept of the Standard Oil combination itself, was the persuasion of strong men to join the alliance and to work together effectively in its management.'[21]

The very features that will make an entrepreneur successful in building a business – vision, self-belief, stubbornness, ego and greed – will often make integration of that business into a large corporation very difficult. However, the best acquisitions are usually those where either the strong-willed entrepreneur can be removed on day one because the acquiring company has a clear plan and its own managers, or where sufficient autonomy can be created such that the energetic founder can continue to thrive in the corporate environment.

The latter was one of Rockefeller's great skills and many of the senior managers of Standard Oil were drawn from the ranks of the founders of the companies he acquired, and who became enthusiastic and entrepreneurial executives.

Cost savings and synergies
Mergers and acquisitions should enable the managers of the combined entity to cut costs and/or capture synergies.

Cost savings, like removing one of two head offices, creating a single finance function, closing factories and re-assigning production capacity, are relatively easy to identify and relatively easy to capture. The main reasons for failure are that the original businesses retain too much of their own infrastructure and the new top management are reluctant to confront them.

Synergies like increased sales or the famous 'leverage the customer base' are much more ethereal, even mythical. Management of the divisions now under unexpected common ownership often exhibit a 'silo' mentality, protect their own turf and refuse to cooperate.

A bank (provider of current accounts) buys an insurance company (provider of motor insurance). 'We will leverage our customer base by cross selling,' says the bank. Well, perhaps they will or perhaps customers will prefer to buy motor insurance from a motor specialist.

The telephone utility buys a music publishing record company. 'We will sell music online to our cell-phone customers,' they say. Fine. But what if those customers want artists from other labels not owned by the music company?

Dedicated teams get the projects done

The process of combining two organisations is very different from normal management and usually requires some dedicated resources. People must take responsibility for establishing a specific timetable and the achievement of well-defined merger goals. Typically this means things like establishing a new organisation structure and putting people into the new jobs.

The process of merger can ruffle many feathers and it is often better to have a full-time process manager – perhaps an outside consultant – who can take a lot of the knocks so as to leave the senior team of the merged entity without a lot of baggage. Research by Deloitte & Touche suggests that a full time role of integration director is a key factor in making combinations work.[22]

Summary

- Building a business through mergers and acquisitions is a core skill for CEOs and they must involve themselves fully in negotiation of transactions and leading the integration process.
- The majority of business combinations fall because of poor integration.
- The least risky deals are 'tuck-in' acquisitions that allow a business to capture the cost savings from consolidation.
- The best negotiators look for win–win solutions.
- Managing the post-deal integrations requires special skills and a dedicated team.

12 Telling the story: communication

*Companies need to impress many audiences if they are to thrive
in terms of operating performance and market value. The CEO
has a leading role in defining a company's image and
managing the communications process. The first 100 days for
a new CEO is a key period in terms of communication.*

Companies that are well thought of will be more successful than
those which are badly regarded or unknown. Companies with a
poor or non-existent image will find it harder to raise capital, to recruit and retain good people, to launch new products and to get
deals done. Companies that sell goods or services to the public need
strong consumer brands. Those which sell to other businesses also
benefit from positive recognition. All companies benefit from having
a 'good name'. In an age when information is instant, the CEO has
to lead and manage the corporate reputation.

The CEO has the role of 'corporate brand manager' and some
people suggest the title of 'chief communications officer' is implicit
in the CEO's job. However, the trend in the 1990s for CEOs to become so high profile that they were more famous than their companies proved to be damaging. It is the company and its products that
should be the star not the person.

Chapter 1 defined the main corporate constituencies whose perceptions have to be informed and managed. Although a company
may employ communications professionals to deal with these groups
it is not possible for CEOs to distance themselves from the process.
The performance of the company's products and services and the
attitude and behaviour of its employees form an important part of
the communications message.

Value of reputation

A company's reputation is one of its most valuable assets. A good reputation leads to:

- better sales to consumers, who will admire the products and service of a well-regarded company;
- better recruitment and retention of staff, who will want to work for a popular company and who will be motivated by factors other than just cash compensation;
- improved share price through a higher rating, which also helps to fund acquisitions;
- easier access to capital from bankers and bondholders, who will require lower interest rates from respected borrowers;
- increased opportunities to achieve mergers and acquisitions, as potential targets will regard the company as partner of choice.

It is a classic virtuous circle, but it has to be managed and will not simply occur by accident. A truly great corporate story will get all stakeholders excited and supportive.

Communication is where all the other elements of the CEO's role come together. The vision and strategy have to be articulated in a way that is convincing and easily understood both inside and outside the business. The company's employees must understand and accept the thinking behind structure and tactics. The prospect of a growing future profit stream will attract investors who will push up the value of the company's stock.

Creating corporate myths

A corporate story is just that – a story. A simple, compelling and convincing narrative that sets a company in context and defines, in an engaging way, where it is going. We all like a simple legend about countries, people, sports teams and film stars. It helps us feel we understand what they are about. It is the same with companies.

Let me give some examples of the way corporate stories can be told in one paragraph. These are not official descriptions – simply my own interpretation.

MICROSOFT

Built by Harvard drop-out Bill Gates from his inspired recognition that software is more important than hardware. Characterised by tough and aggressive business tactics. Pioneered (but did not invent) the concept of the simple graphical user interface Windows. Marketed (but did not invent) the most popular applications like word processing and e-mail. World leader. Unstoppable.

SOUTH WEST AIRLINES

No frills, low cost, point-to-point airline, which is consistently profitable and growing. It benefited from the charismatic leadership of Herb Kellener. Gets better returns than other airlines because of clear-minded focus on cost and can-do corporate culture. Much copied by other low-cost airlines but never bettered. Will grow earnings by continuing to take market share.

DELL COMPUTERS

Started by college student Michael Dell in Texas. Pioneered concept of assembly-to-order and just-in-time manufacturing for PCs. Brilliant user of mail order and the internet. Growing faster than other PC makers. Will continue to find innovative manufacturing solutions.

These are simple stories. Stories that read like Hollywood 'high concept'. But it is their simplicity that gives them strength and resonance with all the corporate constituencies.

The leaders of the companies (Gates, Kellener and Dell) are famous because they built star businesses, not because of themselves. Their ego is less than the corporate ego. The CEO must also be prepared to be storyteller-in-chief, although should avoid the temptation of being the solo star actor as well.

These myths may be brilliant inventions of a public relations 'spin doctor' but they are more likely simply images that have grown over time because of consistent behaviour and communications.

CEO style

Communication is about style as much as substance. *How* a story is told is often as important as the content. All CEOs will have their personal approach to getting the message across. The way a CEO communicates will determine the effectiveness of the message.

Bill Gates is renowned for his e-mails; Jack Welch for his handwritten notes; Tony O'Reilly (ex-CEO, Heinz Corporation) for his after-dinner speeches; Warren Buffett for his annual reports.

It is important to recognise that in communication one size does not fit all. If a CEO really is a poor public speaker, then conference platforms are to be avoided, though it is hard to see how a CEO can be effective without public communication skills.

Some people are delightful lunch companions who will entertain and endear themselves. Others are hard work and meals end up punctuated by long, painful silences. Some 'give good phone', others come across as terse and cold. Whatever the message, CEOs should use those techniques that are tried and tested for them and avoid getting talked into methods they find make them uncomfortable.

There is no shame in CEOs having presentation or media training. They are technical skills to be learned like accountancy, IT or market research. Executives who have been very successful managers might have been able to avoid big presentations and media attention during their careers but if they are appointed as CEO, they come with the job.

In terms of communications style, people need to be consistent. It is disturbing for audiences to face a person who on some occasions is brusque and humourless and on others discursive and entertaining. A switch of styles makes people worry they are being conned or that something is wrong. CEOs need to be honest with themselves about how they most naturally come across and try always simply to be themselves. Acting is for the professionals.

CEOs are themselves a key part of a company's image. Writing in *Marketing* magazine Laura Mazur observed:

> ... Whether they like it or not, chief executives are part of the company's brand equity ... the chief executive's 'brand' communicates what the company stands for.[1]

Communication tools

The main communication challenge for a company and its CEO is serving the needs and expectations of different audiences at the same time. A company has many communications methods available to it but most are audience specific.

The dense, legally defined, financial reports in documents like the Report and Accounts and the 10Ks[2] are required by professional investors but can be off-putting and even negative to employees and customers. The annual report can become a costly exercise in self-aggrandisement. I have on two occasions worked for companies where the cost of the annual report was in excess of the annual profits being reported on. If not checked, they somehow become monsters with a life of their own. And spending too much can often have the opposite of the desired effect by implying corporate waste.

Warren Buffett uses the annual report of Berkshire Hathaway as a vehicle for his investment philosophy and over the years it has become a 'must-read' and much reported annual publication. Sir Martin Sorrell at WPP uses his annual report for an assessment and analysis of the key trends in marketing and advertising and, again, it is a much-used source for other observers of the media scene and is regarded as an annual contribution to intellectual capital.

Of course, both CEOs could simply publish their ideas on their industry or their investment approach at any time they like. The annual report provides a 'peg' or 'hook'.

Internal newsletters detailing progress of the staff softball team may assist in boosting morale, but do little to inform investors, sell more products or engender customer loyalty. Another drawback of the in-house paper is that most of us, as employees, treat it with some scepticism. We regard it as a form of unreliable propaganda. Articles about the social aspects of the company and basic information about new divisions or savings plans are fine but the interview with the boss can often be regarded as a Soviet-style attempt to disseminate the party line.

In practice, a profile of a CEO by a business magazine or an interview about prospects with the *Wall Street Journal* or the *Financial Times* has far more credibility. External features like this reproduced in an internal publication will create a much less cynical response.

The face-to-face meeting is not used nearly enough, as many business leaders find them too time consuming. However, CEOs really do have to be good at public speaking and a company's various audiences will judge the overall business by how well its leader performs in public.

The roadshow to investors is now an established part of most public company routines but the same material can be very interesting to employees and even customers. Well presented, it gives a compelling picture of the company's operations and future prospects. If a CEO performs well in these meetings it creates a very positive climate of morale, as people feel the business is in good hands.

Is e-mail a blessing or a curse? There is no doubt that we all receive (and probably send) too many. It also has the danger that we approach it like a telephone chat – informal, unconsidered, but it remains on the printed record potentially forever, as an increasing number of court cases are demonstrating.

Michael Eisner, the CEO of Disney, has suggested that an electronic time-lock should stop us replying instantly to controversial internal e-mails as we are tempted to reveal our short-term anger in a way that we would not in a letter or memo. Authored late at night in a hotel room after a long dinner, such an e-mail with an ill-considered, ungrammatical and perhaps profane message, can cause irreparable harm to a business relationship in a way that an off-the-cuff rude response at the water cooler never would. At a minimum we all send and receive more information than is required.

The internet comes to the rescue

Most corporate communication is 'push'. That is to say, it is designed for a particular audience and sent to them. The e-mail, the memo, the speech, the video, the brochure, the presentation, the annual report, all are targeted communications.

Someone decides who the communication is aimed at and what it should contain. This usually means that any audience (other than the target) is not very well served by any particular communication and even the target audience will rarely get exactly what they want, having too much or too little detail.

The internet and its close cousin the corporate intranet have changed all this. Vast quantities of information, data and argument can be made available on demand. The user can decide what he or she wants to extract from a web site as and when required. The role of the company is to keep information up to date and to provide good search tools and a logical structure.

Many corporate web sites remain an expensive embarrassment as they simply reproduce off-line printed documents, but increasingly the medium allows stakeholders to extract their own version of the story.

All the raw material of the corporate site – the individual pages – have to be 'owned' by someone who will be responsible for keeping that page up to date. The overall look and feel and function of the site need to be controlled by someone at the corporate centre, but that person is normally much more concerned with how the site works than what it says.

CEOs should look at their own company's sites regularly and make frequent comments. Increasingly it is the most public face that companies have.

Investor relations and the share price

The value of a company's shares is not just a matter of its actual past, present and future cash flows. It's a matter of investor perception. Ultimately investors buy shares because they think other people will want to as well. Investors will buy shares in companies which they think are good at creating a positive image – good at investor relations.

The economist John Maynard Keynes likened the process to a newspaper beauty parade where readers pick the six prettiest girls from hundreds of pictures, the winning reader being the one whose selections most closely matched the opinions of readers as a group.

> It's not a case of choosing those which, to the best of
> one's judgement, are really the prettiest, nor even those
> which average opinion genuinely thinks the prettiest.
> … We devote our intelligences to anticipating what
> average opinion expects average opinion to be.[3]

Thus, it is not just a matter of how a company performs but also of how it is perceived. The investment community actually wants companies to be good at managing their image.

Analysts and investment managers

The front line of opinion on Wall Street or the City is occupied by the analysts. 'Sell-side' analysts work for investment banks and broking firms who make their money from creating transactions in shares. The 'buy-side' work for the investment managers and make their living out of picking winners.

Over the past few years the reputation of sell-side analysts has dropped sharply as they are seen more as marketing executives for their banking employers rather than as genuine, independent, advisers. In many ways this is unfair as some are smart, hard-working and independent people but they are tarnished by the structure in which they operate.

Both groups can be of great value to a CEO as they provide objective feedback on how the company is doing, how the investment community views it and, crucially, what their competitors are up to. Talking to clever and well-informed analysts is the best source of free consulting a CEO can find.

Media relations

A remarkable number of senior executives (CEOs included) are frightened of journalists and wary of media interviews. They make the assumption that journalists have an agenda, are seeking to damage them and are digging for dirt. In fact journalists simply want a good story, be it positive or negative, and have a right to expect CEOs to make themselves available. CEOs are, whether they like it or not, public figures. Being open to media criticism (or praise) is a by-product of the big salary and the corner office.

The British business community is familiar with the story of Gerald Ratner, who brought down his own career and his large family company by making jokes at a public meeting about how some of his jewellery products were 'crap' and that was the reason he could sell them so cheaply. It was a joke he had made several times before but it only became a *cause célèbre* when reported by the media. But the journalists who made it into a story had no malice towards Ratner; they had simply selected an angle that was controversial.

Jack Welch commented on the period shortly after he took over as CEO when he was trying to lead a programme of cultural change:

> The company's mood fluctuated on the bullishness of
> our press clippings and the price of our stock. Every
> positive story seemed to make the organization perk
> up. Every down beat article gave the whimpering cynics
> hope.[4]

CEOs and other senior managers are frustrated by media commentary because they cannot control it. But it is precisely because it is independent that readers give it far more credibility.

Broadly speaking, there are three types of journalist:

- Subject specialists who follow a sector or even a company and will have as much knowledge as a stock market analyst.
- News reporters who will cover a very wide range of subjects.
- Editors who control programmes, newspapers or magazines.

The CEO (even of the largest company) should try to get to know the relevant subject specialists. Like stock market analysts, these specialists can be valuable sources of objective feedback and a mine of information about competitors.

Knowing editors will, at least, allow a company to be given the benefit of the doubt if things go wrong and may lead to more balanced coverage than would otherwise have been the case. But CEOs are mistaken if they think journalists are really their 'friends' and will let them off the hook if errors are made. The agreeable lunch four times a year in which pleasantries and confidences are exchanged is a very minor part of a journalist's working life and the peer pressure of colleagues, editors and competing media will ensure that an acquaintanceship with a company leader will not get that CEO good coverage if mistakes have been made.

Internal relations

Employees are also ambassadors for the business and the corporate message must be clear internally both because of morale and because the staff themselves are an important external communications channel.

More than with any other group, there is the risk of CEOs being branded hypocritical by employees. Exhortations to save costs, for example, will be met with a very negative response if the CEO is felt to be profligate.

Inside a company there is no more powerful or credible internal communication than 'The CEO told me personally that ...' The things people tell their direct reports directly trickle down into an organisation with far more credibility than most written messages.

It is in this area that CEOs can build or destroy a reputation for integrity. If different messages are given to different people, or if CEOs indulges in political intrigue, they will get caught out.

If the message being delivered is unwelcome and the course of action the CEO has chosen unpopular, he or she must be consistent, arguing the case on its merits rather than to trying to 'buy off' disgruntled managers with vague promises. Because businesses are not democracies, politics should play no role. Consultation is legitimate. Conspiracy and compromise are not.

Actions do speak louder than words

CEOs often have to be seen to do things which in themselves are a powerful message. Charles Heimbold, CEO of Bristol-Myers Squibb, comments:

People see that I go out on customer calls with the sales force. They see that when there are devastating ice storms in Quebec I am on the phone right away to find out what has happened to our people, and making sure we're getting emergency supplies up there. They can see that I am as committed to my co-workers and their success as they are.[5]

Early in my own career I worked as a television reporter for the BBC and remember one weekend when we were visited by our boss's boss's boss, the then controller of BBC One, Michael Grade. We were short staffed and dealing with a shipwreck story in the North Sea. Grade offered to help out and do a junior researcher's role to find us a coastguard to interview. He did this with good humour and success. I have no idea if it was a contrived gesture but we all talked about it with admiration for weeks afterwards.

It is not cynical or manipulative for a CEO to consciously decide to take certain actions and to take steps to see that his or her involvement is publicised in an appropriate way. If CEOs really do make a sales call or spend time serving customers or try their hand on the production line, then it is legitimate that these actions are communicated.

If the impression is given that the CEO is simply play-acting at involvement, then a negative and cynical response is to be expected from the organisation. But if it is a genuine attempt to help out and learn, then the action deserves to become part of the corporate mythology.

Managing the board

Most CEOs report to a board, combining executive and non-executive directors. Indeed, one of the reasons CEOs have so much power is that they are frequently the only person in the company who does not really have a 'boss', instead being held to be responsible to a group of people.

Even where the board has a chairman, this individual is usually a part-time non-executive and is there more to manage the board process than to give the CEO instructions.

But boards can fire CEOs and the main lesson is 'no surprises'. Successful and long-tenured CEOs will make sure that their fellow directors know the good and bad news long before it is revealed in a board meeting.

Crisis response

The communications skills of a company and its CEO are really tested when things go wrong.

Tylenol discovered poisoned packages on retailers' shelves. Perrier had reports of benzene in its mineral water. Exxon spilt millions of gallons of crude oil into the sea. Firestone tyres on Ford Explorers failed and the cars rolled over.

A major crisis should always involve the CEO personally, if only because more junior managers will often have the urge to cover up and keep their heads down rather than confronting the problem head-on. The public and the media look for courage, honesty and rapid response when things go wrong. It is a time when a CEO must lead from the front.

The lessons of successful political leaders apply in times of crisis:

- Admit there is a problem even if you do not yet have a solution. When British Labour prime minister Jim Callaghan responded 'Crisis. What crisis?' to news of a collapse in the British pound, he did not endear himself to voters who put the Conservatives in office for the next thirteen years.
- Be seen to be personally involved. Visit the site of the incident. President George W. Bush had a poor start to the September 11 terrorist attacks when he was literally flying in circles for some hours, but recovered by showing concern and direct involvement in the days after.

- Take decisive action quickly. If reports come in of contamination in a food or medicine, do you risk losing a month's sales by pulling the product off all the shelves in the country or do you risk losing the brand's lifetime reputation by hoping it is an isolated incident and keep it selling only to discover other problems in days to come? It is always better to take the moral high ground, even if it damages short-term profits.

A crisis is a time when the CEO absolutely has to lead the communications effort and be seen to be the chief spokesperson.

The first 100 days

The most important time for a new CEO to communicate well is the period just after they take over as the boss of a company. It's the time when a new corporate story can begin.

Presidents, prime ministers and elected mayors are now all caught on the idea of how they handle the 'first 100 days'. People, the media and voters judge leaders on quick results. No political leader can now escape the post-100-days analysis of success or failure. The same is true for the new CEO.

The first 100 days are often vital to politicians in establishing a basis for subsequent re-election. For new CEOs, they define a personal and corporate image that will help them do (and in some cases, *keep*) their job.

Some CEOs come to a company from other jobs in other businesses and might, reasonably, be expected to have little inside knowledge. Others may have been in the organisation all their working lives and may be stepping up from a COO or CFO position. However, whatever the background, the start of the period is a huge opportunity for change and should be approached this way whatever the background of the new CEO.

How to approach those 100 days?
Broadly speaking there are three phases:

1 Find out what is going on.
2 Develop a story.
3 Tell the story.

In the first month new CEOs are well advised to keep their heads down and avoid any public statements about what they are planning to do. They need information. This means meeting senior managers face to face. And meeting key customers and suppliers. Even if someone has been COO for years and has just stepped into the top job, they need to see the main stakeholders in the context of their new role. If only as a courtesy, people should feel they have had some input into the new CEO's agenda before they read about it in a newspaper.

The second month is a time to articulate the new statement of the vision (even if the vision remains the same) and to develop and test out the strategy and to settle on any structural and management changes. If senior people are going to be hired or fired, it should happen by now.

The final month should be devoted to getting the story across to all audiences.

Having a good story is vital to a CEO as they have to get a lot of people all moving in the same direction. The story has four main elements:

1 History and context.
2 The imperative. The need to do something.
3 The point of inflection. The moment of change.
4 The vision and destination.

History and context
All companies have a history. Even brand-new start-ups have the his-

tory of the founders themselves. That history is a key part of the story as it gives the listeners – the corporate constituencies – a context within which to judge the company's future prospects.

No politician would seriously hope to run a country or a city without a good grasp of its history and heritage. The same is true of a company. Senior managers, particularly the CEO, should understand how their company, indeed their industry, came into existence. Did their industry replace an earlier one? How does their industry fit into the overall economy? What are the historical reasons for the shape and structure of their industry? Within the context of the industry what are the roots, core values, etc. of their own business?

COCA-COLA AND SANTA CLAUS

The Coca-Cola Company has invested in an excellent three-storey exhibition in its home town of Atlanta, Georgia, which traces the roots of the business from a pharmacist's invention of a new tonic drink in 1886. (Did you know that Coke's advertising department invented the modern image of a red-cloaked Santa Claus?)

Going around the exhibition (they get you to pay $6 to watch their commercials!) I was struck by how many high-quality young managers must have entered the company having been first intrigued by these exhibits. And how motivating it must be for staff to have such a clear and engaging picture of their company's history and rationale.

All companies should be like Coke and have a clear and compelling story about where they came from and how they got to be the way they are.

The imperative

A new CEO needs to tell his or her organisation that some one thing is the high priority that needs addressing. It can be some form of threat, or an opportunity – a change in legislation, a new competitor, the chance to enter a new market, the need to cut costs or the need to expand. Whatever it is, it should be an excuse for a new, energy-generating corporate crusade. An imperative to action they can all focus on.

The appointment of a new CEO is an ideal moment to conjure up just such a call to arms. It's a way to galvanise the enthusiasm of employees and to capture the imagination of investors.

The point of inflection
To introduce their new regime CEOs need a 'hook'. They must seize upon a single event which crystallises the new programme – or seems to. It can be a product launch, the first set of results, a key board meeting, a strategy away-day or an AGM.

The corporate legend needs to be able to point at a specific event and say, in effect, 'the future started here'. A company needs to be able to tell itself, 'It was then we saw the truth about our past and our competitive situation. It was then we all understood and bought into the new vision.'

The vision and destination
This is the company vision and the strategy described in Chapters 3 and 4. It must be expressed in a language that everyone can immediately understand.

If, after 100 days, all a CEO can come up with is 'We are going to keep doing what we always did', people are likely to feel let down, even if the past has been very successful. It is fine for a new CEO to say, 'We have been doing very well and we will stick to our knitting,' but some new elements must be added to show that the company is moving forwards. People must be given a sense of momentum.

Using those 100 days well
In the first 100 days a new CEO does not have performance to show in terms of profit numbers, and will therefore be judged more by

actions and approach than on results. Actions in these early days become highly symbolic.

If the imperative is about sweeping away an overblown bureaucracy, then things like selling the company jet and/or abolishing the directors' fleet of chauffeur-driven limousines will send a powerful message. Firing senior managers who are known to have become passengers and promoting well-regarded young talent sends a message about meritocracy. A quick acquisition of a competitor or a major contract win speaks to expansion plans. A move to a new corporate office with better facilities and a better location is the opposite of the cost-cutting message but may do wonders for corporate self-confidence and morale depending on context.

New CEOs are not in a popularity contest. They are not running for public office. They have already 'won' the election. They are expected to take the hard decisions and do things to make their term a success.

New CEOs must use the first 100 days to impose their will as most organisations try to carry on as they always have. Interviewed by the magazine *Market Leader*, the CEO of Cadbury Schweppes, John Sunderland, commented:

> When a new CEO comes in with his own particular
> ideas and ways of doing things the organization tends to
> duck and hope these new ideas will vanish into the
> ether so they can carry on doing things the way they
> were.[6]

Not all CEOs succeed in their early communications. When Jack Welch was appointed at GE in 1981 he made a speech to Wall Street analysts. He recalled in his autobiography:

> It was my first public statement on where I wanted to
> take GE. The analysts arrived expecting to hear a

detailed breakdown of the financial numbers. Over a
20-minute speech, I gave them little of what they
wanted and quickly launched into a qualitative
discussion around my vision for the company. At the
end, the reaction in the room made it clear that this
crowd thought they were getting more hot air than
substance. I left the hotel ballroom knowing there had
to be a better way to tell our story. Wall Street had
listened, and Wall Street had yawned. I was sure the
ideas were right, I just hadn't brought them to life.[7]

Welch goes on to explain that it took him some years to find a way
of communicating his vision but in the end he came up with a dia-
gram based on three circles which led to his famous 'fix, sell or close'
dictum to ensure GE was number one or two in its chosen markets.

No matter how excellent a CEO's programme is, it will fail unless
it is well communicated.

Summary

- The CEO must lead the development and promotion of a
  positive corporate image but must avoid the temptation of a high
  personal profile. The star of the show should be the company,
  not the boss.
- A positive image has benefits in all areas of activity including
  sales, recruitment and stock rating.
- The CEO must be active in internal communication so everyone
  'knows the story' and must be available and responsive to
  external questions. 'Hiding' from journalists and analysts will
  normally produce negative interpretations.
- Managing the first 100 days for a new CEO is a crucial stage in
  developing a positive corporate image.

Conclusion

This book does not end with a neat summary or a simple to-do list. There are no easy answers or basic recipes to follow. There is neither a magic commercial spell nor a management 'silver bullet'. The conclusion is that the role of the CEO is multi-faceted and complex and that the job requires a balancing act to be done well.

The constantly moving environment of a business means that priorities must alter and successful leaders must be flexible. CEOs who believe they have all the right answers will almost certainly fail as they are too rigid in the face of new circumstances. Perhaps THE defining feature of the best CEOs is that they start each day with the questions 'What has changed, what can I do to make this business better and are our customers still happy?'

Everyone else in a company has a specific set of tasks and goals. What makes it so difficult and so interesting for CEOs is that they must worry about the unknown and the ill defined. What does all the information about current trading really mean, what might competitors do next and what does the future hold?

The CEO gives the business its sense of direction and energy. When a CEO goes home at night feeling the day was a good day and things went well, the only certainty is that tomorrow the doubts and questions will start all over again.

From a personal perspective, writing this book has been a fascinating and valuable exercise. It forced me to read the ideas of business leaders and management thinkers and to look at recent commercial history. Also it provided the excuse for many conversations with colleagues about how companies *really* work. Despite all this I am still not able to come up with a description of what makes the perfect CEO but perhaps it comes down to four broad traits:

- Making the complex simple through articulating a clear vision, providing a sense of direction and developing a robust fact-based strategy reflecting the true economics of the business.
- Building a strong organisation by hiring good people, defining their tasks and motivating them by giving autonomy.
- Getting things done by being passionate about implementation and holding people to account.
- Using capital well by extracting the maximum cash from the business, picking the best projects and making deals work by good integration.

Success is not just about CEO charisma and making inspiring speeches. Being tough as a CEO is not about firing people and slashing costs. It is being tenacious about keeping up standards and serving customers well. When people used to say 'a CEO took no prisoners' it often meant they were very tough on costs and fired a lot of people. Increasingly it means they have an unbending focus on operational excellence.

This book promotes the proposition that effective CEOs transform their organisations into enterprises. If I had to come up with a simple formula to show this it would be:

$$\text{ENTERPRISE} = \text{ENTHUSIASM} + \text{EXECUTION.}$$

Enthusiasm is about giving the whole business and all the people who work in it a sense of purpose and direction through exciting goals and inspiring communication. The restless search for something new and better.

Execution is about making things happen. It is having the right people in the right places, putting in the systems to monitor performance and getting cash out as a result.

For a CEO to have the enthusiasm without the execution is like having the bow without the arrows. You need both to get the desired result.

Given this book's title, it is simply too tempting not to end by re-calling the USS *Enterprise*'s Captain Kirk and his signature split-infinitive command from *Star Trek* 'to boldly go'. It may be pure Hollywood but it does capture what leading an enterprise is all about. It is the willingness to take risks and to try new things.

An enterprise is always starting afresh. It is not a predictable or-ganisation. It greets the future with relish, not reservations. It con-fronts change rather than retreating into routine. The role of the CEO is to calculate the risk of alternative paths and find ways to mit-igate the effects of failure. It is about travelling hopefully rather than arriving and about making all the people with you enthusiastic for the journey.

Notes

Part I **Evolution of the CEO**

1 *Daily Telegraph*, 19 Dec. 2002, p. 22 (for WorldCom, Enron, Tyco); *Business Week*, 23 Dec. 2002, p. 49 (for Vivendi).
2 *Financial Times*, 20 Dec. 2002, p. 19.
3 *Eurobusiness*, Sept. 2002, p. 32.
4 *Business Week*, 23 Dec. 2002, p. 49.
5 *Financial Times*, 18 Dec. 2002, p. 13.

1 **What is a business?**

1 Joan Magretta, *What Management Is*, HarperCollinsBusiness 2002, p. 17.
2 David Gross, *Forbes Greatest Business Stories of all Time*, John Wiley & Sons 1996, p. 54.
3 *Fortune*, 9 Dec. 2001, p. 20.
4 *Market Leader* (Journal of the Marketing Society), 14 (Autumn 2001), p. 20.
5 Jeffrey Garten, *The Mind of the CEO*, Penguin 2001, pp. 184–5.
6 *Fortune*, 21 Jan. 2002, p. 20.
7 Stern Stewart & Co., the global consulting firm; web site http://www.sternstewart.com.
8 *The Economist*, 9 March 2002, p. 76.

2 **What is a CEO?**

1 *The Economist*, 9 March 2002, p. 3.
2 Benjamin Franklin, *Autobiography of Benjamin Franklin (1731–1759)*, Dover Publications 1996, Ch. 9.

3 *Red Herring*, Feb. 2002, p. 100.

4 *Daily Telegraph*, 25 Feb. 2002, p. 1.

5 *Oxford Dictionary of Quotations*, rev. 4th edn, Oxford University Press 1996, p. 428, speech to Saint-Cyr cadets, 9 Aug. 1819.

6 Frederick W. Taylor, *Principles of Scientific Management*, Dover Publications 1998 [1911], p. 6.

7 *Evening Standard*, 7 Nov. 2001, p. 36.

8 *The Economist*, 22 June 2002, p. 83.

9 *Financial Times*, 12 May 2003, p. 1.

10 *The Business*, 12 May 2002, p. 1.

11 Stern Stewart, web site http://www.sternstewart.com.

12 Alfred P. Sloan, *My Years with General Motors*, Doubleday 1990 [1963].

13 Alfred Rappaport, *Creating Shareholder Value*, The Free Press 1986.

14 *The Economist*, 4 May 2002, p. 81.

15 *Fortune*, 18 Nov. 2002, p. 48.

16 Ibid., p. 16.

17 *The Economist*, 4 May 2002, p. 81.

18 Ibid., p. 11.

19 Ibid.

20 *Financial Times*, 3 May 2002.

21 *Sunday Telegraph* Business Section, 22 Sep. 2002, p. 7.

22 *Forbes Global*, 17 March 2003, p. 24.

23 *Financial Times*, 16 July 2002, p. 15.

Part II **The role of the CEO**

1 From Theodore Levitt, 'Marketing Myopia', *Harvard Business Review*, July–August 1960; reprinted in Henry Strage (ed.), *Milestones in Management*, Blackwell 1992, pp. 75–97. Copyright © 1960, Harvard Business School Publishing Corporation; all rights reserved. Reproduced by permission.

2 Alfred P. Sloan, *My Years with General Motors*, Doubleday 1990 [1963].

3 Louis V. Gerstner Jr, *Who Says Elephants Can't Dance?*, HarperCollins 2002, p. 235.

3 Defining the business: vision

1 From James Collins and Jerry Porras, 'Building Your Company's Vision', *Harvard Business Review*, Sept. 1996, p. 74. Copyright © 1996, Harvard Business School Publishing Corporation, all rights reserved. Reproduced by permission. (Quote from Henry Ford with Samuel Crowther, *My Life and Work*, Garden City Publications Company, 1922, p. 73.)

2 Ibid.

3 Bob Thomas, *Building a Company*, Hyperion 1998.

4 Daniel Gross, *Forbes Greatest Business Stories of all Time*, John Wiley & Sons 1996, p. 110.

5 Robert Slater, *Saving Big Blue*, McGraw-Hill 1999, p. 109.

6 Ibid., p. 110.

7 *Sunday Telegraph* Business Section, 29 Sept. 2002, p. 4.

8 From Joan Magretta, 'Why Business Models Matter', *Harvard Business Review*, May 2002, p. 88. Copyright © 2002, Harvard Business School Publishing Corporation, all rights reserved. Reproduced by permission.

9 *The Times*, 14 Nov. 2002, p. 35.

10 Sam Walton with John Huey, *Made in America*, Doubleday 1992, p. 25.

12 Ibid., p. 50.

4 Setting clear goals: strategy

1 Michael Porter, *Competitive Strategy*, The Free Press 1980; the original figure is at p. 4.

2 John Love, *McDonald's: Behind the Arches*, Bantam Books 1995, p. 153.

3 Daniel Gross, *Forbes Greatest Business Stories of all Time*, John Wiley & Sons 1996, p. 194.

4 Jack Welch, *Jack: What I've Learned Leading a Great Company and Great People*, Warner Books 2001, p. 448.

5 Ensuring accountability: structure

1 Frederick W. Taylor, *The Principles of Scientific Management*, Dover Publications 1998 [1911].

2 Daniel Gross, *Forbes Greatest Business Stories of all Time*, John Wiley & Sons 1996, p. 55.

3 *The Economist*, 11 May 2002, p. 63.

4 Ibid.

5 Louis V. Gerstner Jr, *Who Says Elephants Can't Dance?*, HarperCollins 2002, p. 86.

6 Finding talent: people

1 *USA Today*, 20 Feb. 2002, p. 2B.

2 Eva Innes et al., *The 100 Best Companies to Work for in Canada*, Financial Post 1986.

3 From Nicholas Ind, *Living the Brand*, Kogan Page 2001; quoted in *Market Leader*, 15 (Winter 2001), p. 36.

4 *Fortune*, 20 Jan. 2003, p. 27.

5 http://www.greatplacetowork.com.

6 Marcus Buckingham and Curt Coffman, *First Break all the Rules*, Simon & Schuster 2001, p. 28.

7 Larry Bossidy and Ram Charan, *Execution: The Discipline of Getting Things Done*, Crown Business 2002, p. 92.

8 Jack Welch, *Jack: What I've Learned Leading a Great Company and Great People*, Warner Books 2001, p. 162.

9 *Forbes*, 28 Oct. 2002, p. 42.

10 Ibid., p. 38.

11 Welch, *Jack*, p. 192.

12 Louis V. Gerstner Jr, *Who Says Elephants Can't Dance?*, HarperCollins 2002, p. 97.

13 *The Economist*, 16 Nov. 2002, p. 86.

14 *Smart Business*, Jan. 2002, p. 90.

15 *Management Today*, Nov. 2002, p. 54.

7 Delegating authority: tactics

1 *Fortune*, 26 May 2003, p. 26.

2 Louis V. Gerstner Jr, *Who Says Elephants Can't Dance?*, HarperCollins 2002, p. 230.

3 *Forbes Global*, 11 Nov. 2002, p. 45.

4 Daniel Gross, *Forbes Greatest Business Stories of all Time*, John Wiley & Sons 1996, p. 98.

5 Ibid.

6 Larry Bossidy and Ram Charan, *Execution: The Discipline of Getting Things Done*, Crown Business 2002, pp. 25 and 27.

7 Tom Peters and Bob Waterman, *In Search of Excellence*, Harper & Row 1982, p. 318.

8 Jim Collins, *Good to Great*, Random House 2001, p. 123.

9 Jack Welch, *Jack: What I've Learned Leading a Great Company and Great People*, Warner Books 2001, p. 261.

10 Gross, *Forbes Greatest Business Stories*, p. 186.

11 Ibid.

12 From Robert Kaplan and David Norton, 'The Balanced Scorecard', *Harvard Business Review*, Jan.–Feb. 1992. Copyright © 1992, Harvard Business School Publishing Corporation, all rights reserved. Reproduced by permission.

13 From Michael Jensen, 'Corporate Budgeting is Broken – Let's Fix It', *Harvard Business Review*, July 2001, p. 96. Copyright ©

2001, Harvard Business School Publishing Corporation, all
rights reserved. Reproduced by permission.

14 Welch, *Jack*, p. 386.

15 From David Garvin, 'Building a Learning Organization',
Harvard Business Review, July–Aug. 1993. Copyright © 1993,
Harvard Business School Publishing Corporation, all rights
reserved. Reproduced by permission.

16 *Market Leader*, 14 (Autumn 2001), p. 20.

17 *Forbes*, 28 Oct. 2002, p. 38.

8 Operating effectively: cash

1 Judi Bevan, *The Rise and Fall of Marks & Spencer*, Profile Books
2001, pp. 4, 178 and 202.

2 *Business Week*, 28 Jan. 2002, p. 28.

3 *Business Week*, 18 Nov. 2002, p. 89.

4 *Fortune*, 30 Dec. 2002, p. 83.

5 Michael Dell with Catherine Fredman, *Direct from Dell*,
HarperCollinsBusiness 1999, p. 22.

9 Moving forward: change

1 *Daily Telegraph*, 25 April 2002, p. 1.

2 Charles M. Farkas, Philippe de Backer and Allen Sheppard,
Maximum Leadership 2000, Orion Business/TEXERE Publishing
1999, p. 166.

3 Louis Gerstner in *The Times*, 14 Nov. 2002, p. 35.

4 *The Business*, 13 Oct. 2002, p. 25.

5 From Eric McNulty, 'Welcome Aboard but Don't Change a
Thing', *Harvard Business Review*, Oct. 2002, p. 38. Copyright ©
2002, Harvard Business School Publishing Corporation, all
rights reserved. Reproduced by permission.

6 *Fortune*, 16 Sept. 2002, p. 46.

7 Louis V. Gerstner Jr, *Who Says Elephants Can't Dance?*, HarperCollins 2002, p. 76.

8 *Financial Times*, 15 March 2002.

9 *Sunday Times*, 20 Oct. 2002, p. 37.

10 Nelson Mandela, *A Long Walk to Freedom*, Little, Brown 1994, p. 492.

11 From Larry Hirschhorn, 'Campaigning for Change', *Harvard Business Review*, July 2002. Copyright © 2002, Harvard Business School Publishing Corporation, all rights reserved. Reproduced by permission.

12 *Financial Times*, 20 Feb. 2003, p. 12.

13 *Fortune*, 16 Sept. 2002, p. 42.

14 Ibid., p. 47.

15 Jack Welch, *Jack: What I've Learned Leading a Great Company and Great People*, Warner Books 2001, p. 182.

16 Gerstner, *Who Says Elephants Can't Dance?*, p. 50.

17 Farkas, de Backer and Sheppard, *Maximum Leadership 2000*, p. 154.

10 Picking winners: investment

1 *Fortune*, 18 Feb. 2002, p. 21.

2 *Fortune*, 14 Oct. 2002, p. 93.

3 Ibid.

11 Managing transactions: deals

1 Matthias M. Bekier et al., 'Mastering Revenue Growth in M&A', *McKinsey On Finance,* Summer 2001, p. 4.

2 Ibid.

3 *Financial Times*, 12 Feb. 2002, p. 18.

4 *Sunday Times* Business Section, 2 June 2002, p. 12.

5 *Financial Times*, 25 March 2002, p. 22.

6 *Forbes*, 28 Oct. 2002, p. 27.

7 *The Economist*, 26 Oct. 2002, p. 81.

8 *Financial Times*, 23 Dec. 2002, p. 17.

9 *Wall Street Journal*, 5 Sept. 2001, p. 1.

10 *Financial Times*, 12 Feb. 2002, p. 18.

11 *Financial Times*, 25 Feb. 2002, p. 22.

12 *Fortune*, 24 Dec. 2001, p. 100.

13 *Forbes*, 15 April 2002, p. 58.

14 *Business Week*, 7 Oct. 2002, p. 69.

15 Judi Bevan, *The Rise and Fall of Marks & Spencer*, Profile Books 2001.

16 *Sunday Telegraph*, 25 Nov. 2001, p. 10.

17 *Wall Street Journal Europe*, 27 Dec. 2002.

18 *The Times*, 25 June 2002, p. 29.

19 For example Peter B. Stark, *It's Negotiable*, Pfeiffer & Co 1994; Roger Fisher et al., *Getting to Yes*, Arrow 1997; Herb Cohen, *You Can Negotiate Anything*, Lyle Stuart 1980; William Ury, *Getting Past No*, Random House 1992.

20 *Wall Street Journal*, 24 Jan. 2002.

21 Daniel Gross, *Forbes Greatest Business Stories of all Time*, John Wiley & Sons 1996.

22 Deloitte & Touche, *The Integration Director: Man or Superman?*, May 2002.

12 Telling the story: communication

1 *Marketing*, 8 May 2003, p. 20.

2 Regular reports required by the Securities and Exchange Commission in the USA.

3 John Maynard Keynes, *The General Theory of Employment, Interest and Money*, Harcourt Brace Jovanovich 1964 [1936], p. 156.

4 Jack Welch, *Jack: What I've Learned Leading a Great Company and Great People*, Warner Books 2001, p. 172.

5 Thomas Neff and James Citrin, *Lessons from the Top*, Random House 1999, p. 172.

6 *Market Leader*, 14 (Autumn 2001), pp. 30–34.

7 Welch, *Jack*, p. 107.

Sources

In preparing this book I have tried to seek out the best ideas on how businesses work, what it takes to be a good CEO and how the job can be done well.

A huge amount has been published on the technical aspects of management and finance, but not that much on general management. Many of the CEO books are more 'How to become CEO' or 'How I ran XYZ Corp' rather than how to approach and do the job. Much of the writing is on specific aspects of corporate leadership such as strategy or finance or marketing. There is surprisingly little on the CEO role itself.

From the perspective of someone running a company (or hoping to), much of the best published inspiration comes from business biographies and histories. It is true that many of these are one-sided, self-promoting, *post-facto* rationalisations. However, some are excellent documents and often contain the best lessons of business.

Lou Gerstner's own account of the turning round of IBM, *Who Says Elephants Can't Dance?*, and Jack Welch's memoir of his time at GE, *Jack: What I've Learned Leading a Great Company and Great People*, provide lessons from people who were very successful. I also very much recommend Daniel Gross's *Forbes Greatest Business Stories of all Time* for those seeking a compendium of fascinating insights. Some of the most entertaining business reads also have management insights, such as *Barbarians at the Gate* by Bryan Burrough and John Helyar and *The New, New Thing* by Michael Lewis.

I have learned more from this type of practical book than from the vast and somewhat overwhelming library of academic works on the theory of business, which often presents contradictory views.

However, major works do emerge which can both stimulate and provide powerful frameworks for analysis. I still believe that Michael Porter's 1980 classic *Competitive Strategy* is the best analytical toolbox a CEO can have. Peter Drucker's *Practice of Management* and Frederick Taylor's *Principles of Scientific Management* have well-deserved icon status. *In Search of Excellence* by Tom Peters and Robert Waterman and the more recent *Good to Great* by Jim Collins are full of fascinating, research-based insights.

Before it appears between hard covers, much of the leading-edge management thinking appears in the *Harvard Business Review*, which over the years has a remarkable track record of showcasing major new ideas.

Real, practical business examples abound in the daily, weekly, monthly and quarterly press. As will be obvious from the notes, I have made extensive use of *Fortune*, which has a special focus on describing corporate strategies, together with *Forbes and Business Week*, *The Economist*, the *Financial Times* and the *Wall Street Journal*.

Newspapers and magazines

Business 2.0; published by AOL Time Warner; web site:
    http://www.business2.0.com
Business Week; published by The McGraw-Hill Companies; web site:
    http://www.businessweek.com
Financial Times; published by Pearson plc; web site:
    http://www.ft.com
Forbes; published by Forbes Inc.; web site: http://www.forbes.com
Fortune; published by AOL Time Warner; web site:
    http://www.fortune.com
Harvard Business Review; published by Harvard Business School; web
    site: http://www.hbsp.harvard.edu
Management Today; published by Haymarket; web site:
    http://www.clickMT.com

Market Leader; published by The Marketing Society; web site:
   http://www.marketing-society.org.uk
Marketing, published by Haymarket; web site:
   http://www.marketingmagazine.co.uk
The Economist; published by Economist Newspapers Ltd, web site:
   http://www.economist.com
USA Today; published by Gannett; web site:
   http://www.usatoday.com
Wall Street Journal; published by Dow Jones & Company; web site:
   http://www.wsj.com

Note: The publisher has endeavoured to ensure that all URLs referred to in this book are correct and active at the time of going to press, but can make no guarantee that a site will remain live or that the content is or will remain appropriate.

Books and articles

This is not in any way an exhaustive list but includes sources I have found useful and interesting.

Bekier Matthias M. et al., 'Mastering Revenue Growth in M&A',
   McKinsey On Finance, Summer 2001, pp. 1–5
Bevan, Judi, *The Rise and Fall of Marks & Spencer*, Profile Books 2001
Bossidy, Larry and Ram Charan, *Execution: The Discipline of Getting
   Things Done*, Crown Business 2002
Buckingham, Marcus and Curt Coffman, *First Break All the Rules*,
   Simon & Schuster 2001
Burrough, Bryan and John Helyar, *Barbarians at the Gate: The Fall of
   RJR Nabisco*, Harper & Row 1990
Cassidy, John, *Dot.com*, Penguin 2002
Champy, James and Michael Hammer, *Reengineering the Corporation*,
   HarperCollinsBusiness 1993

Charan, Ram, *What the CEO Wants You to Know*, Crown Business 2001

Coffey, Elizabeth, *10 Things that Keep CEOs Awake*, McGraw-Hill 2003

Coffman, Curt and Gabriel Gonzalez-Molina, *Follow this Path*, Warner Business Books 2002

Cohen, Herb, *You Can Negotiate Anything*, Lyle Stuart 1980

Collins, James and Jerry Porras, 'Building Your Company's Vision', *Harvard Business Review*, Sept. 1996, pp. 65–77

Collins, James and Jerry Porras, *Built to Last*, Century Business 1996

Collins, Jim, *Good to Great*, Random House 2001

Dell, Michael with Catherine Fredman, *Direct from Dell*, HarperCollinsBusiness 1999

Drucker, Peter, *The Practice of Management*, Harper & Bros 1954

Farkas, Charles M., Philippe de Backer and Allen Sheppard, *Maximum Leadership 2000*, Orion Business/TEXERE Publishing 1999

Fisher, Roger et al., *Getting to Yes*, Arrow 1997

Fox, Jeffrey J., *How to Become CEO*, Hyperion 1998

Garten, Jeffrey, *The Mind of the CEO*, Penguin 2001

Garvin, David, 'Building a Learning Organization', *Harvard Business Review*, July–Aug. 1993, pp. 126–39

Gates, Bill, *Business @ The Speed of Thought*, Penguin 1999

Gerstner, Louis V., Jr, *Who Says Elephants Can't Dance?*, HarperCollins 2002

Gross, Daniel, *Forbes Greatest Business Stories of all Time*, John Wiley & Sons 1996

Hirschhorn, Larry, 'Campaigning for Change', *Harvard Business Review*, July 2002, pp. 98–104

Ind, Nicholas, *Living the Brand*, Kogan Page 2001

Innes, Eva et al., *The 100 Best Companies to Work for in Canada*, Financial Post 1986

Jensen, Michael, 'Corporate Budgeting is Broken – Let's Fix It', *Harvard Business Review*, July 2001, pp. 96–102

Kanter, Rosabeth Moss, *The Change Masters*, Simon & Schuster 1983

Kaplan, Robert S. and David P. Norton, 'The Balanced Scorecard', *Harvard Business Review*, Jan.–Feb. 1992, pp. 43–51

Kaplan, Robert S. and David P. Norton, *The Strategy-Focused Organization*, Harvard Business School Press 2001

Katzenbach, Jon R., *Real Change Leaders*, Random House 1995

Keynes, John Maynard, *The General Theory of Employment, Interest and Money*, Harcourt Brace Jovanovich 1964 [1936]

Kotter, John P., *A Force for Change*, Free Press 1990

Kuo, J. David, *Dot.bomb*, Little, Brown 2001

Levitt, Theodore, 'Marketing Myopia', *Harvard Business Review*, July–August 1960; reprinted in Henry Strage (ed.), *Milestones in Management*, Blackwell 1992, pp. 75–97

Lewis, Michael, *The New, New Thing*, W. W. Norton 2001

Love, John F., *McDonald's: Behind the Arches*, Bantam Books 1995

Magretta, Joan, *What Management Is*, Profile Books 2002

Magretta, Joan, 'Why Business Models Matter', *Harvard Business Review*, May 2002, pp. 86–92

Mandela, Nelson, *A Long Walk to Freedom*, Little, Brown 1994

McNulty, Eric, 'Welcome Aboard but Don't Change a Thing', *Harvard Business Review*, Oct. 2002, pp. 32–40

Neff, Thomas and James Citrin, *Lessons from the Top*, Random House 1999

Peters, Tom and Bob Waterman, *In Search of Excellence*, Harper & Row 1982

Porter, Michael, *Competitive Strategy*, The Free Press 1980

Porter, Michael, *On Competition*, The Free Press 1988

Rappaport, Alfred, *Creating Shareholder Value*, The Free Press 1986

Slater, Robert, *Saving Big Blue*, McGraw-Hill 1999

Sloan, Alfred P., *My Years with General Motors*, Doubleday 1990 [1963]

Stark, Peter B., *It's Negotiable*, Pfeiffer & Co. 1994

Stewart, James B., *Den of Thieves*, Simon & Schuster 1991

Strage, Henry (ed.), *Milestones in Management*, Blackwell 1992

Sun Tzu, *The Art of War*, trans. Samuel B. Griffith-Thomas, Oxford University Press 1971

Taylor, Frederick W., *The Principles of Scientific Management*, Dover Publications 1998 [1911]

Thomas, Bob, *Building a Company*, Hyperion 1998

Ury, William, *Getting Past No*, Random House 1992

von Clausewitz, Karl, *On War*, Penguin Classics 1982 [1832]

Walton, Sam with John Huey, *Made in America*, Doubleday 1992

Welch, Jack, *Jack: What I've Learned Leading a Great Company and Great People*, Warner Books 2001

Wolf, Michael J., *The Entertainment Economy*, Penguin 1999

Index

Numbers in *italics* indicate Figures; those in **bold** indicate Tables.